What do people say about Perfected Mind Control?

"I basically learned the mindset of how one would strongly persuade someone on a long term basis and also the mindset of doing so in a non-destructive manner."
~ David K.

"I read it with some friends - they are interested already - I won't recommend it to many people - only open minded and evolved souls."
~ James D.

"i think you should be locked up for ever!! fools like your cult are and will be distroyed!!"
~ Charles M

"I appreciated this book so much, and look forward to further data in this field... "
~ K. H.

"...the reason I bought PMC was because I have a project I am working on and I want to turn the cast into a cult."
~Raul G.

"I purchased PMC over the weekend and have read it thoroughly twice now and I feel I am the one who has been hypnotized. I feel like I am 2 people and I am not the one in control. i feel completely changed and craving more. i don't know what "more" is, but i am completely overwhelmed with the need for more."
~ Bobbie

"The book as it stands is good; very specific..."
~Scott S.

D0988881

"It's a work of art and science working in harmony. Only people responsible enough, open minded, happy with life, willing to share themselves, willing to learn new things about them- selves,and honest should read this book.. "
~Fritz M.

I give this high marks. I believe you have hit the nail squarely on the head. I enjoyed reading the material and shall enjoy implementing much of same. At my discretion by all means.
~Mike

... excellent. ...I'm selfish, I want to keep it to myself. If someone else is too lazy to read it, more power for me. I'll make sure that the members of my cult understand the need to stay away from this material, while I continue to learn and benefit from it...
~Master

Perfected Mind Control

by Dantalion Jones

ISBN 1440475830
ISBN-13   9781440475832

Contents

Open Letter to the Reader

Okay, before we dive into Perfected Mind Control (**PMC**) there's likely a few things you need to know.

First, when you read "mind control" in this book there are two definitions, one narrow and one broad.

The narrow definition of "mind control" is the ability to control and influence other peoples thoughts and behaviors.

The broad definition of "mind control" is the ability to control thoughts and behaviors in general including and especially within ones self.

Both will apply when I describe **Perfected Mind Control** or **PMC**.

This illumination began after many years of research and application of various persuasion technologies and having numerous successes and failures. Eventually I asked myself a few questions that led me to where you are now, reading this book.

These questions may shock you to even consider the answer.

• What are the **beneficial** aspects of mind control?

• What is missing in the narrow definition of mind control that would increase the beneficial aspects?

• What are the biggest challenges for the people using mind control on others that limit their success?

• How can the two words "mind control" be changed from something people avoid to what people appreciate and accept?

Think about it.

If you're like most people you will begin to think I'm an evil madman bent on world domination. While I admit that world domination does have a romantic appeal, I'm simply not willing to devote the time and energy to make that happen.

What I do want is to have people really ask serious questions about what they think, believe and perceive.

Let me also explain that I'm releasing this book with a certain degree of hesitation.

Why? Near the end of this book I've included an eight processes that can be used on a subject that **will** induce very powerful changes. You should be warned that anyone who uses them is taking full responsibility in what happens.

There is no end to the trouble that can happen if someone simply uses the processes without first applying them to themselves.

Let me repeat that.

There is no end to the trouble that can happen if someone simply uses the processes without first applying them to themselves.

If you are motivated by unrestrained adolescent urges for sex, money and power it's very likely you're going to create a stock of subjects that you are unable or unwilling to control.

Just paint a picture of you in a crowded restaurant with someone special while you are being yelled at by a coked out subject that you should have never taken on in the first place!

If you apply these processes in some professional setting, like teacher of counselor, it's very likely you could imagine seeing yourself standing on a hard-wood floor looking eye-level to see a judge banging a gavel at your own sentencing hearing.

With luck you get the picture.

Apply these processes on yourself first! If you do you may discover that the it's good information but using it on others is simply not worth your effort. You may also find some excitement in sharing **PMC** and its increased flexibility that you'll be living.

To some, especially to some men, "mind control" represents a salvation from sexual frustration, poverty and self doubt. For those men this might be a tough ride because the majority of work you'll have to do is on yourself and not on the numerous mind control prospects* out there.

But you're welcome to take the ride and see where it leads you.

One of the main differences between the **PMC** model of mind control and what we traditionally think of "cult mind control" is that **PMC** *doesn't* want to convert the world and everyone in it. **PMC** is only interested in recruiting the brightest, most positive, adventurous prospects* to go through the various **PMC** processes to become a full initiate*.

You'll find that the *right* prospects make your "cult" a fun and enjoyable adventure. The *wrong* prospects will, piss you off, alienate members from each other, incites infighting, steal time, money and resources, lie, and cause you to quickly reevaluate what you are doing.

For the long run you'll find it easier and more fun to start with only two or three dedicated initiates* into your "inner circle" as you build your house*.

Hope you have a fun adventure!

Yours Truly,

Dantalion Jones

*Definitions:
"**Prospect**" is someone whom you don't know is

suited for recruitment. *"**Recruit**"* is a prospect going through the **PMC** processes at the end of the book. *"**Initiate**"* is someone who has already gone through the **PMC** processes. *"**House**"* is, for lack of a better term, the name you'll use to call your cult.

Introduction

What possible benefit is there in promoting Mind Control?

In order for one to learn to create the most happiness in their life they need to know how to do it with the least possible amount of effort. That only comes from learning how to handle power and that can only come from creating the opportunity to have it.

The facts are that there is no outside source of power. It's not limited in any way. There is always enough power available and more. The only limitation is the mind of the user and their ability to connect with the universe. The **Perfected Mind Control** processes are simply one vehicle to experience that power, whether one uses it on others or on themselves.

The only unit of measurement for power is influence. For that reason the only way to gain it is to have successful applications of influence; each one bigger than the one before it. First one tries the **Perfected Mind Control** processes on themselves and then on others.

Power has no ethics. It's neither good nor bad and acts like a magnifying glass. So, if the self is flawed and weak power will magnify the flaws and weaknesses. The effect is obvious when you see people crash and burn when they get a minuscule amount of power. Again, another reason to apply the **Perfected Mind Control** processes on yourself first.

Mind control is just one avenue of power. Many will find that it's not their cup of tea. That's okay. There are plenty of other ways of expressing it.

The most amusing fact is that power is not all that it's cracked up to be. One who is skilled at using power (and Mind Control) will find that the more power they have the less they will use it. The ultimate artistic expression of use of power is to find the smallest possible effort to get the greatest possible influence.

When the **PMC** project was first conceptualized in my mind it came in a flash and was followed by a cascade of insights.

I had some experience with cults and their various processes and found them rigid in their belief systems and overly paternalistic.

Originally it was hoped that this book would be a completely coherent explanation of **Perfected Mind Control**. What resulted instead was a outline and a compilation of essays that are vital to **PMC** as it's conceptualized.

The goal of this work is to help you create a cult-like "house" of obedient and, most importantly, *happy* followers who rely on your wisdom, fun, and inspiration.

Your followers should be fully functional members of society that live this strange mind control life style to prove that it works for them.

So, **Perfected Mind Control** pretty shocking.

On the downside I've been told by people close to me that this work is anywhere from "shocking" to "blasphemous".

On the other hand I've also been told by people that they "get it" and it's not *really* about controlling other, but a cloaked way of giving control to the reader without having to use it on others.

The best advice is to grab your chair firmly with both hands and read it all the way through. When you begin to read the **PMC** Processes you should do so having gotten a lot of rest and be fully prepared to challenge everything you think is right and true.

Good Luck.

Dantalion Jones

The Thought Paper That Inspired "Perfected Mind Control".

Before going deeper into the concept of Perfected Mind Control I'll present to you a "thought paper" on a concept that compares old style mind control as described by Robert Jay Lifton way back in 1961.

With **PMC** I want to develop a system of mind control that does all or most of the end results of traditional mind control but is absent of all the "coer- cive" elements that are described in Robert Jay Lifton's Eight Point Model of Thought Reform.

So, you see, I'm walking a fine line here but per- haps there's something that could have some prom- ise.

Let's get started.

Terminology note: Today Mind control or brain- washing in academia is commonly referred to as co- ercive persuasion, coercive psychological systems or coercive influence. The short description below comes from Dr. Margaret Singer professor emeritus at the University of California at Berkeley the acknowledged leading authority in the world on mind control and cults. This document, in substance, was presented to the U.S. Supreme Court as an educational Appendix on coercive psychological systems in the case Wollersheim v. Church of Scientology 89-1367 and 89-1361. The Wollersheim case was being considered related to issues involving abuse in this area.

> *The Goal of "Perfected Mind Control" (**PMC**) is to completely minimize or eliminate any perception of coercion while expanding the subjects ability to choose. Is it mind control? Yes. It is designed so that the subject gains greater control of their mind and a higher degree of flexibility in their responses. Is **PMC** coercive? You be the judge. It is also mind control in the narrow definition in that the "operator" or cult leader has control of the direction of where the subjects thoughts and behaviors can go. The difference is that there is no failure if the subject does not move in that direction. Instead it's framed as an experiment that the subject can try again at a later time.*

Coercion is defined as, "to restrain or constrain by force..." Legally it often implies the use of PHYSICAL FORCE or physical or legal threat. This traditional concept of coercion is far better understood than the technological concepts of "coercive persuasion" which are effective restraining, impairing, or compelling through the gradual application of PSYCHOLOGICAL FORCES.

A coercive persuasion program is a behavioral change technology applied to cause the "learning" and "adoption" of a set of behaviors or an ideology under certain conditions. It is distinguished from other forms of benign social learning or peaceful persuasion by the conditions under which it is conducted and by the techniques of environmental and interpersonal manipulation employed to suppress particular behaviors and to train others. Over time, coercive persuasion, a psychological force akin in some ways to our legal concepts of undue influence, can be even MORE effective than pain, torture, drugs, and use of physical force and legal threats.

The Korean War "Manchurian Candidate" misconception of the need for suggestibility-increasing drugs, and physical pain and torture, to effect thought reform, is generally associated with the old concepts and models of brainwashing. Today, they are not necessary for a coercive persuasion program to be effective. With drugs, physical pain, torture, or even a physically coercive threat, you can often temporarily make someone do something against their will. You can even make them do something they hate or they really did not like or want to do at the time. They do it, but their attitude is not changed.

> *The phrase "against their will" implies that an individual has a clear preset intention. The truth is that very **very** few people have thought out their intentions to the degree that something else cannot be suggested. As a central understanding of Perfected Mind Control this concept allows for only the rare few who*

actually have a "will" to be excluded from any influence.

This is much different and far less devastating than that which you are able to achieve with the improvements of coercive persuasion. With coercive persuasion you can change people's attitudes without their knowledge and volition. You can create new "attitudes" where they will do things willingly which they formerly may have detested, things which previously only torture, physical pain, or drugs could have coerced them to do.

> *The key to **PMC** is to present all new concepts in terms of "learning" and all form of rejection in terms of "judgment and prejudice"*

The advances in the extreme anxiety and emotional stress production technologies found in coercive persuasion supersede old style coercion that focuses on pain, torture, drugs, or threat in that these older systems do not change attitude so that subjects follow orders "willingly." Coercive persuasion changes both attitude AND behavior, not JUST behavior.

COERCIVE PERSUASION
vs Perfected Mind Control

Coercive persuasion or thought reform as it is sometimes known, is best understood as a coordinated system of graduated coercive influence and behavior control designed to deceptively and surreptitiously manipulate and influence individuals, usually in a group setting, in order for the originators of the program to profit in some way, normally financially or politically.

The essential strategy used by those operating such programs is to systematically select, sequence and coordinate numerous coercive persuasion tactics over CONTINUOUS PERIODS OF TIME. There are seven main tactic types found in various combinations in a coercive persuasion program. A coercive persuasion program can still be quite effective without the presence of ALL seven of these tactic types.

PURPOSE AND TACTICS OF 'PERFECTED MIND CONTROL"

The purpose of **PMC** *is to liberate the mind from automatic and unconscious responses that are painful. The tactics are designed to have a minimum of judgment and moralization to them so to cause minimal discomfort. The tactics emphasize choice and self-awareness with a constant invitation to leave and rejoin in the learning.*

TACTIC 1. **The individual is prepared for thought reform through increased suggestibility and/or "softening up,"** specifi- cally through hypnotic or other suggestibility- increasing techniques such as: A. Extended audio, visual, verbal, or tactile fixation drills; B. Excessive exact repetition of routine activities; C. Decreased sleep; D. Nutritional restriction.

In order for anyone to accept a new concept, yes, they must be "softened up". However with **PMC** *this is not done by wearing them down. Instead one simply is pointing out the ways in which a persons responses and choices are automatic and how the automatic response* **limits** *their ability to choose.*

Perfected Mind Control – www.MindControl101.com

TACTIC 2. **Using rewards and punishments, efforts are made to establish considerable control over a person's social environment, time, and sources of social support.** Social isolation is promoted. Contact with family and friends is abridged, as is contact with persons who do not share group-approved attitudes. Economic and other dependence on the group is fostered. (In the forerunner to coercive persuasion, brainwashing, this was rather easy to achieve through simple imprisonment.)

> More subtle punishments have greater power. Stunned glaring silence for example or merely looking at the floor with shaking the head have a strong impact on the internal feelings of the subject. Another way of accomplishing that silently is by raising the eye brows while moving the head slightly forward and accompanied by a smirk. Also, simply asking in a "Dr. Phil" type tone "How has that been working for you?" will allow the subject to compare their automatic behavior with their ideal response.

TACTIC 3. **Disconfirming information and nonsupporting opinions are prohibited in group communication**. Rules exist about permissible topics to discuss with outsiders. Communication is highly controlled. An "in-group" language is usually constructed.

> Keeping the discussion "on topic" is important to **PMC**. That does allow for debate and to a point debate should be encouraged. The central point of **PMC** is on freedom and flexibility

of choice. If debate turns the topic away from that the subject should be acknowledged for contributing and asked to return to the topic. If the distraction continues the subject should be compassionately told that they aren't yet ready to learn and that it's not their fault and asked to return at another time or simply remain silent and listen.

TACTIC 4. **Frequent and intense attempts are made to cause a person to re-evaluate the most central aspects of his or her experience of self and prior conduct in negative ways.** Efforts are designed to destabilize and undermine the subject's basic consciousness, reality awareness, world view, emotional control, and defense mechanisms as well as getting them to reinterpret their life's history, and adopt a new version of causality.

> *Perfected Mind Control instead focuses first on the subject to re-evaluate **any** aspect of their life in **any** new way. The degree of success is measured by how the subject responds positively to this new (but perhaps even minor) insight. Thus making a paved path ready for any further insights.*

TACTIC 5. **Intense and frequent attempts are made to undermine a person's confidence in himself and his judgment, creating a sense of powerlessness.**

> *As in pointing out times when their behaviors did not match up to their stated values. While this does have some limited value the emphasis of **PMC** is on the **reward** that*

comes from greater choices and increased flexibility.

TACTIC 6. **Nonphysical punishments are used** such as intense humiliation, loss of privilege, social isolation, social status changes, intense guilt, anxiety, manipulation and other techniques for creating strong aversive emotional arousals, etc.

In Perfected Mind Control this is completely avoided by making the only punishment silence or shaking the head slightly while looking at the ground. Silence without judgment so that the judgment can only be inferred.

TACTIC 7. **Certain secular psychological threats [force] are used or are present:** That failure to adopt the approved attitude, belief, or consequent behavior will lead to severe punishment or dire consequence, (e.g. physical or mental illness, the reappearance of a prior physical illness, drug dependence, economic collapse, social failure, divorce, disintegration, failure to find a mate, etc.).

In Perfected Mind Control the only psycho- logical threat is not being one of "us". But also making it okay to not be one of "us".This puts the subject into one of two other categories
"them" and "undecided". Old Mind control methods made it only us/them while the the "undecided" allows the subject more ease to return to "us". For the people employing Perfected Mind Control this system has a bigger picture. It creates a dichotomy for the "us" to rally against. And those who are "undecided" can still be in the loop of communication.

Perfected Mind Control – www.MindControl101.com

*In Perfected Mind Control people will be asked and **encouraged** to leave the group to find out what more is "out there". Their choice to return or not is always respected. Those who return will do so with more commitment and those who leave will still be in the loop of communication.*

Another set of criteria has to do with defining other common elements of mind control systems. If most of Robert Jay Lifton's eight point model of thought reform is being used in a cultic organization, it is most likely a dangerous and destructive cult. These eight points follow:

Robert Jay Lifton's Eight Point Model of Thought Reform

1. **ENVIRONMENT CONTROL.** Limitation of many/all forms of communication with those outside the group. Books, magazines, letters and visits with friends and family are taboo. "Come out and be separate!"

*Perfected Mind Control **discourage** limitations such as "move in with our commune" by making it hard to do unless under the right circumstances or with only proper preparation. By doing this only the most committed will attempt to do so while others are given a model to aspire. Perfected Mind Control also **encourages** exposure to outside information within the context of "...comparing it to what you now know with us". By doing this the illusion of choice is always present.*

2. **MYSTICAL MANIPULATION.** The potential

convert to the group becomes convinced of the higher purpose and special calling of the group through a profound encounter / experience, for example, through an alleged miracle or prophetic word of those in the group.

Perfected Mind Control will emphasize that the only higher purpose is understanding that sense of right and wrong unconsciously filters what they are able to learn. Therefore morality is a hindrance to learning. And learning is the key to ultimate freedom and the flexibility to enjoy and deal with anything that life gives you.

3. **DEMAND FOR PURITY.** An explicit goal of the group is to bring about some kind of change, whether it be on a global, social, or personal level. "Perfection is possible if one stays with the group and is committed."

*In Perfected Mind Control (**PMC**) the demand for purity is replaced by the demand to **truly** learn. To Truly learn can only be done by testing and putting aside judgment.*

4. **CULT OF CONFESSION.** The unhealthy practice of self disclosure to members in the group. Often in the context of a public gathering in the group, admitting past sins and imperfec- tions, even doubts about the group and critical thoughts about the integrity of the leaders.

*The **PMC** model replaces confession of wrongs with exploration of wants, needs and desires. This dynamic will automatically reveal* *what the subject thinks they are doing wrong or want to improve without the overt sense of guilt or shame. Guilt and shame fall into the category of "Bad Thing".*

5. **SACRED SCIENCE.** The group's perspective is absolutely true and completely adequate to explain EVERYTHING. The doctrine is not subject to amendments or question. ABSOLUTE conformity to the doctrine is required.

For Perfected Mind Control the only truth that adequately explains everything is that "We experience the world only by perception. Therefore if we can gain control of our perception we gain control of our world."

6. **LOADED LANGUAGE.** A new vocabulary emerges within the context of the group. Group members "think" within the very abstract and narrow parameters of the group's doctrine. The terminology sufficiently stops members from thinking critically by reinforcing a "black and white" mentality. Loaded terms and clichés prejudice thinking.

New vocabulary will emerge in any field of personal exploration and should be expected. **PMC** *is no different.*

7. **DOCTRINE OVER PERSON.** Pre-group experience and group experience are narrowly and decisively interpreted through the absolute doctrine, even when experience contradicts the doctrine.

PMC*s only "doctrine" is the commitment to self-exploration. All other fields of study are* *permissible. This allows the subject to define their own doctrine and discard it when needed to reform a new one.*

8. **DISPENSING OF EXISTENCE.** Salvation is possible only in the group. Those who leave the group are doomed.

*Instead of only two catagories of "saved" and "doomed" **PMC** allows for a minimum of three catagories "Those who get it." "Those who don't want it." and "Those who don't know about it." this allows those who leave the group to fall **only** into the category of "Those who don't know about it." and thus permits them to return. The "Those who don't want it." category is only used as a reference point or for those people who advocate the opposite of freedom and flexibility.*

Perfected Mind Control – www.MindControl101.com

Perfected Mind Control: Starting at the Beginning

Understanding

Why is the beginning important?

Because at the end of book you'll find an appendix of **PMC** processes that can be used with individuals to create any response, behavior or emotional state you desire. Before applying these processes it's important to understand the main obstacle that would prevent the operator for achieving success: the mindset of the operator.

You may dare to run out and perform these **PMC** processes on people without the proper preparation but I warn you, the result is likely that you will have bitten off much more than you can chew.

In the words of Spiderman *"With great power comes great responsibility."* So consider yourself warned.

So what is the beginning of **PMC**?

Most people will speculate that **PMC** starts with the message the operator or cult leader will present. His doctrine of the cult or movement.

That's not where to begin.

The beginning is in the *mindset* of the operator or so-called leader. How he looks at his life, his beliefs about himself as they relate to his mission and others and the mental processes he uses to take action.

In the old style cult the cult leader simply used his conviction, a little charm as he doled out rewards and punishments. These rewards and punishments were based on how closely the recruit followed the doctrine.

The old cult mindset (bad thing) is based on right-or-wrong thinking and actions of others. There was very little acceptance given except for those who completely towed the party line.

This old process is filled with **HUGE** limitations, namely *morality.*

As an example how can someone understand a cult as extreme as the Heavens Gate cult who committed group suicide in order to "get to the next level and board the mother space ship"?

Most people will simple explain such behaviors by saying "They were crazy."

But what if they weren't?
What if they really did "go to the next level"? Then they would be right and you would be wrong!

Here is the catch, **whenever you use your morality to understand something you are unconsciously bringing up reflexive responses that limit your ability to sincerely understand.**

In other words, most people unconsciously default to judgment/morality when we are attempting the process of understanding. When that happens there is no looking deeper. The walls are up to anything different and "They were crazy" makes sense. But if they weren't crazy it might require something different to understand. It might require examining something that is too uncomfortable to think about.

That is the difference.

The **PMC** operator has the ability to put aside all values and judgment in search of understanding.

So the first quality of mindset in the **PMC** *operator is the* **understanding that moralizing and judgment hinder true understanding** *and he will attempt to be aware of when moralizations are taking place, in himself and others.*

So taking understanding as the lead, the operator next greatest mindset resource is **Patience.**

Patience for the operator comes from having a clear outcome. "Outcomes" are defined as goals that are **positive, measurable and under the control of the operator.** Anything that is not **under the control of the operator** falls into the category of wishes and hopes and the operator is advised to ignore them.

With an understanding of outcomes, the rest is a matter of time hence the need for patience. The operator has an understanding that while the end outcome has value the **next most recent outcome is the *most* important outcome.** This creates a combination of having a big picture of what your long-term outcome is and the next step toward reaching it. Every smaller outcome should fit perfectly like a jigsaw puzzle to form the larger outcome you desire.

This mindset prevents the hurried rush of urgency that is often accompanies unrestrained youth.

The Mystery of Silence
Silence, as you'll learn, creates a unique sense of mystery. The **PMC** operator does well to apply the following rules when considering his outcomes:

Conceal your intentions.
Being open with your intentions invites people who will obstruct, steal and hijack what you've intended.

Demonstrate through actions never through argument.
Telling people what you do will invite the thought that you are a braggart and you risk boring others with stories of your accomplishments. If these stories are remembered they are likely to be retold with skepticism. People remember what is done and build stories and mythologies around your actions by combining their story with their own emotions. Use this to your advantage and let other people speak of your actions.

Always say less than necessary.
There is a mystery that comes from the "strong si-

lent" type. Saying something outright can be forgotten but if you allude to something, even something you know will happen, when it occurs the mystery will be confirmed.

This does not mean that you are unemotional or cold. Instead you behave as if you know something that most people don't know or something that they shouldn't know.

Make what is difficult seem easy.

This again adds to the mystery of the operator. There are several ways that this can be done, one such way is guile like sleight of hand or prestidigitation. One method using guile is to allude to an unforeseen incidence as if you did knew about it before hand but this should be done sparingly. Another such way to make the difficult seem easy is skill and experience and has the strongest impact.

With this strong emphasis on mystery it does not mean that you act completely unaccessible. Instead, **what you teach** should be treated as a mystery. What you know is for few to discover and only those rare individuals who are ready can learn it. This will allow you to mix in any social circle, tease, laugh, flirt and cajole while the mystery of your knowledge and understanding follows you like compelling lover.

Conviction

Conviction is a fairly simple concept. It means that you are certain of what you are doing and why you are doing it. Conviction means that you are so convinced that what you are doing it right, justified and good that it compels you act. Strong conviction will compel you so powerfully to face any opposition without fear or hesitation. Conviction will also cause you to ignore any personal fears or anxieties.

With that as a definition of conviction ask yourself if there is anything you feel that strongly about? If there is the dive into it and use it as a resource.

If you don't yet have something that motivates you to that level of conviction it's not too late. Think about the things that you love to do and be active in. remember times when committed yourself to do something simply because you knew it was right and felt good.

If you ever want to watch two people empowered by their conviction speaking to the public just watch any old videos of Rev. Billy Graham or Adolf Hilter. Ignore the message and turn off the sound. Just watch them. Both are compelling speakers that are hard to ignore.   That is the level of conviction you might want to aspire.

As a simple exercise give encouragement to some-one using only the power of your conviction. Meaning let them know that you know their plans are worth while, important and needed. Tell them you believe in what they say, and what they want to do. Be ab-solutely convinced that they can do. You'll be sur-prised how positively they will respond.

Focus
If you have a strong conviction that what you are doing is right. You won't need too much help to build your focus. But let's assume you have no idea what focus really is.

First, your sense of focus is to be used and demonstrated whenever you are with someone who could be a prospect, recruit or initiate. When you are in their presence there should be nothing more than them on your mind.

Your goal is to create an experience for them (you're a guru remember?) that they are the most important person in the world at that moment in time. Like the exercise above you'll be surprised at how positively they will respond.

In order to do this let's take a look at how most of our lives are like.

First, there is no secret to the fact that no matter who you are shit is going to happen. You are going to have to pay bill, feed your belly and think about where the next dollar is coming from... this is just a part of life.

Your ability to focus and get what you want with a prospect, recruit or initiate can be directly effected by all of these things *if you let them.* Even if they never come up in conversation. If those distracting details are on your mind during a conversation you will not impact anyone to the degree that you could.

What you have to do at those moment is inten-tionally *put aside everything that could distract you from paying attention to that person.* When you do that nothing else is important and it will af-fect them in a very powerful way.

To exercise this skill just remember meeting someone who inspired you to move forward into ac-tion. Relive the feeling of having a renewed energy just from meeting and talking with them. That is what you want to be able to do with others.

Winning no matter the outcome; The God Complex

The God Complex is my favorite subject and so I hope I do it justice. It's also referred to at "Supreme Strategy".

The God Complex has absolutely nothing to do with a growing sense of infallibility and megalomanical behaviors.

What makes up the God Complex is really a perspective that is far more distant than your next outcome.

Let's face it. With every goal you have a possibility of failure. That's just life. It does happen and it will happen.

But if you incorporate any possible failure into your "big picture" and find a way so that you can benefit from it there will never be a disappointment or surprise. This will allow you to reevaluate what you are doing and make changes. These changes can be in how you look at things, your tactics to achieve your outcome and even your outcomes themselves.

Most people "fail" only because they invest too much of themselves in their success so that when it falls short they are devastated. Some never recover. However if they realize failure is possible and incorporate it... should it happen all they do is continue on with their business.

They have a bigger picture of themselves, Life, and their goals.

The result is they are more flexible to respond to what life throws them. Nothing surprises them except 1) when someone truly "gets it" or 2) when someone who should "get it" doesn't. They are kinder to themselves and to the people around them because they feel in control **no matter what the situation.**

When you have this right you realize that it's not really failure, it's only feedback and with any feedback you can modify your plan and go on.

Let me give you an example.

Bob and Jerry both like the idea of using **PMC** to create a "house" of their own. So they learn what they can, find prospects and recruits and initiate a few members into their houses.

One initiate of each house becomes dissatisfied after a conversation with their family and just quickly leaves and drops all contact. Finally both Bob and Jerry get a concerned call from their former initiates trying to reconcile what happens in the house with what their family is telling them.

Jerry responds by going on the defensive not answering calls and considers counter suiting. His time and energy begins to be consumed by his former initiate.

Bob, on the other hand, knows that this happens and is prepared for it. Instead of getting defensive he has a brief conversation with his initiate right from the start. He say "Let me just first say based on what you just told me I think you have every reason to do what you're doing and you have my support. This is completely your decision and I can't stand in your way. I want to make every possible effort to make your transition as easy as possible. If you need some things you left here you can pick them up or I can have them delivered to you. If you need some recommendations from us or a referral ... you've got it... and if that's what you decide... I completely understand and there is no hard feelings. I know your family cares about you and wants the best for you. You're certainly old enough to make those decisions now on your own."

Bobs former initiate seemed placated and Bob tells the members of his house to help her but to keep any conversation about the activity that happens, and has happened, in the house closed to any former initiate, in other words secret.

Bob had a bigger view of his house and the people in it. He knew these things happen and knew how to deal with them. He made it so that no matter what happens it's a win and supportive of his house and the people in it.

Perfected Mind Control – www.MindControl101.com

The Values of Perfected Mind Control

Most cults live by a set of values and beliefs. From these beliefs evolve a set of behaviors and rituals.

PMC is only slightly different in this regard.

Because **PMC** values *flexibility, a sense of possibility and a sense of wonder* this leaves the users of **PMC** a **much** wider range of responses than Olde Style Cults that insist on conformity through coercion.

The reason that *flexibility, a sense of possibility and a sense of wonder* are important come from the basic premise that the more choices one has the more freedom they can enjoy. If you have one option you have no choice at all. If you have two choices you're in a dilemma, If you three or more choices you have greater and greater freedom.

As an example, a person with a chocolate compulsion has no freedom. She can either eat the chocolate or suffer the cravings. But if she is given the option of being indifferent toward chocolate she has a third option; the option to say 'no' and not suffer.

PMC differs form Olde Style Cults in that this degree of freedom is to extend both externally to the world around you and internally to your thoughts, emotions, reactions and behaviors.

Granted, there are people who are very uncomfortable with having to make choices and taking responsibility for themselves at this level and, as you'll see, **PMC** has a place for them. Yet, there's little doubt that once one is exposed to this concept and gone through the MPC Processes and let go to make their own choices they will eventually settle on a lifestyle that suits them. And because of their exposure to the vast array of possibilities offered by **PMC** they will more easily be able to develop a life style that truly suits them.

One might argue that flexibility (i.e. more freedom) is given at the cost of security. In the **PMC** paradigm security is the result of more freedom. This includes freedom on how to respond to situations.

The Old Style Cult Mindset vs. Perfected Mind Control

This chapter needed to be written about a few thousand years ago when cults began.

I guess it's better late than never.

If you read so far it might not completely surprise you to know that one of my goals is to take all the negative reaction out of the words "cult" and "mind control".

To do that a major change within "cults" and in "mind control" have to be made.

Perhaps I'm an idealist and am expecting too much but what can be done is apply that ideal to Perfected Ming Control and hope the rest of the world catches up.

Here are some of the differences that **PMC** demonstrates:

The External Enemy of Old Cult Mind Set vs. Internal Limitations to Joy

This is the biggest and perhaps the most significant difference between **PMC** and the Old Cult Mind Set (OCMS).

It's doesn't take a lot of research to find out how pain is used as a coercive tool to get mental and behavioral compliance in cults.

If you are forming a **PMC** "house" any use of pain, guilt, shame in **PMC** is eliminated to whatever extent possible . The basic **PMC** philosophy is that all suffering is the result not of the external environment but **how one interprets the external environment**. Therefore the only enemy that should be looked at first is internal and not external.

Convert the Many of Old Cult Mind Set vs. Convert Only the Few Qualified

Most cults want to convert the world. Bullshit!

A **PMC** operator establishes what he is teaching is **not** for the world. In fact in order to qualify to take part in the **PMC** process people must qualify and be patient in taking part in the processes in order to gain more enjoyment in life.

The operator should think of only building his house slowly one person at a time with only the most qualified prospects. A small house of two or three stable recruits is much easier to manage and more enjoyable than a the chaos of managing an extended network of thousands.

That doesn't mean a large organization can't be done. But the operator must work slowly within his/her limits.

Save the World of Old Cult Mind Set vs. Get More Out of Life

That's pretty simple. **PMC** is not about saving the world. It's about getting more out of life and sharing that with the **right** people.

Old Style Cults have a strong emphasis on saving the world. This is easy to understand when the cult is helping you feel so good. But **PMC** requires some caution in this matter. It is completely impractical to do **PMC** on everybody, in spite of how much everybody would benefit. **PMC** demands that you think smaller and apply it first and foremost to yourself and your immediate surroundings.

PMC is an exclusive, not inclusive cult. So saving the world is out of the question. By letting only the right people in you have a higher level of quality control, it's easier to keep free of public scrutiny, and you're able to get more out of life when you only have the RIGHT people around you.

Motivation by Fear/Guilt/Shame of Old Cult Mind Set vs. Motivation by Reward/Pleasure

Going through the **PMC** processes you'll see that the real emphasis is on pleasure, not **BAD THINGS**. Using Fear/Guilt/Shame is a **BAD THING**.

Keep away from bringing about guilt and shame. This can be very hard for some to avoid, so a strong emphasis will continue to be on applying the **PMC** to yourself to get the most flexibility within yourself.

Grow Fast of Old Cult Mind Set vs. Grow Patiently

Believe me, a small group is much easier to control than a big one. It's always best to start off with only one or two good house members and make sure that **everyone** is clear on what to look for in a new house member. By growing very patiently you will make sure that everyone is reading from the same page. You will also weed out those people whose ambitions can try to take the lead.

This can be done by making most of the activities of the house fun oriented instead of problem oriented. By doing this potential recruits can be brought in to see how they respond. If they are enjoying the participation and activities they can be included further. If they are depressed, gossipy, jealous or monopolize house time or resources simply don't invite them back.

"This is not a cult" of Old Cult Mind Set vs. "Sure this is a cult"

I love this part and I'm including it only because I love to shock people. But I'll leave this for you to decide if you want to keep it.

By admitting to the cult-like aspects of **PMC** you

are forcing people to examine their own assumptions. That a basic component of **PMC**.

"Everyone Should Know" of Old Cult Mind Set vs. Only The Select Should Know

With luck you've figured out that **PMC** is exclusive. People are introduced because they seem right and ready to join. Even then, they have to go through the **PMC** processes to be a member of the "house".

So it's important to only talk about it at the right times and with only the most trusted people. This quality of secrecy will add to the appeal of joining for many people.

The Teacher vs. The Guru: A Lesson in Cult Distinctions

Let's make a clear distinction between a teacher and a guru.

A teacher gives knowledge. A guru creates experience.

Teachers are common. Gurus are rare.

A teacher is a job.
A guru is an experience.

Needless to say you want to be a guru. You DON'T want to be teacher.

This doesn't mean that you won't teach classes. The difference is in the presentation. In fact, teaching classes will be core of how you get recruits. It is through your presentation and your passion that you distinguish yourself as a "guru". ***

One obvious way you can do that is by your appearance; wearing a unique piece of jewelry or all white or all dark clothing or clothing that is contemporary but unique in appearance.

On a deeper level the guru has the ability to lead the imagination, hypnotize with his words and enthrall with the passion of his belief. (Remember what you read earlier about conviction?)

In the words of another master persuader and guru in his own right, Mark Cunningham, "You don't want to be a teacher, you want to be a person from whom people want to learn." and therein lies the difference. By being vague and alluding the mysterious you can create an anticipation that people cannot easily verbalize, causing even more mystery!

Your greatest assets in being a guru are your passion for your message and always saying less than needed. These two qualities create a profound sense of mystery as if you know so much more than you dare speak of.

Silence is best understood by never being too direct with your intentions. Instead of saying outright how you wish someone to respond or behave you can use metaphor while bringing to bare all your enthusiasm for the emotions behind the story.

As an example instead of telling your prospect or follower to outright set with you and talk you can say something like "There's a real excitement that comes when someone realizes that that something is about to happen. In that moment your become aware of everything around you and at the same time you focus in on what's right in front of you. That's when you know you're ready to learn something. You know? Do you think you can build that excitement for a moment while we talk?"

You'll note that various gurus have a very minimal use of the pronouns "I" and "me". Instead they'll say "we". Using the first person pronouns should be done with a degree of humility and even a degree of embarrassment. "I" speaks of ego and it's best to minimize it's use in writing and giving public presentations.

*** It is not advisable that you teach a class as a college instructor before becoming aware of the institutions conducts of behavior as well as the term *"en loco parentus"*. Classes held in bookstore, churches and some adult education facilities can be easy to schedule and arrange.

Who is your best Mind Control Prospect?

Here is something that worth commenting on:

Free translation of an article published in the "Daily Medicine" a weekly Swedish magazine targeting health professionals and the public:

> It is a myth that those ending up in the claws of unhealthy cults aresearching people with psychiatric problems. The majority of people ending up in cults are healthy people with an idealistic trait, stable economy and family backgrounds. They have been actively recruited and not searched and signed up with the cult because of any personal interest and as a choice of their own free will. That is to say - they have been "persuaded" to join.

While one might believe that the unstable are easy to control, they are NOT!

Being able to catch is not that same as being able to control.

Plenty of desperate men have built tormented lives for themselves based on the premise that the woman drunk on pills and crying in the corner at the party was an easy pick-up. What they find is the misery has many far-reaching tentacles.

This is true of Perfected Mind Control as well. A strong cult with a self supporting infrastructure is based on recruiting only healthy qualified prospects. The indoctrination process itself will also weed out the unstable personalities.

In order to do this effectively, the **PMC** operator should live by the motto "There's a lot of fish in the sea. Don't pick the ones floating on the surface just because they're easier to catch."

By contrast healthy people may require more effort but the end result is more predictable more pleasant and less painful for everyone involved.

The benefits of having a mentally healthy recruits are:

- more predictable
- the **PMC** processes are effective and they notice a benefit
- they are less subject to playing "victim/savior/persecutor" roles and siphon energy from group resources.
- they are less subject to uncontrollable phobias and anxiety
- more likely to have a stable income

A Healthy prospect has the following qualities:

- physically active

- adventurous
- spontaneity that demonstrates a degree of risk taking
- a mild degree of secretiveness
- need for approval
- a history of stable relationships and jobs

Signs of an unhealthy prospect:

- lot's of prescriptions for psychiatric drugs
- a history of family abuse
- a history of suicide attempts or self mutilation
- alcohol and drug abuse
- insecure, the type the projects problems that aren't there or finds insult when none was intended
- jealousy
- compulsive behaviors
- pathological liars

You should never hesitate to **ex**clude someone from going through the recruiting process and eventually joining your "house". You must be very discriminative and patient.

What you'll find is that if you have a full life with enough social interactions **and you pay attention** you'll start to recognize healthy and unhealthy types.

There are also some great technologies that can help you qualify your prospect as suitable recruits. The best of which is simple handwriting analysis. I'm not going to go into that in detail but you can find a huge amount of resources and books that will help you in this area.

Also by asking open ended questions you will get a lot of good information about your prospect and they will feel more involved and pay attention to you.

Some of your open ended questions can be:

What was your most adventurous experi- ence?

If I were to ask you about the most troubling time in your life, how would tell me you dealt with it?

When you think of the people you've been most attracted to what you find they have in common?

What were your parents like? Did your father ever call you "princess"?

The Decision Survey
At the very end of this book is a survey tool that you can use to get some VERY good information about your prospect. It should be used only **after** you've agreed that they qualify. You'll learn how to use the survey information to help better frame your presentation to each prospect and whom you might want to exclude.

The main point you should leave with having read this chapter is that it's better to have only a few suitable recruits (meaning pleasures) that a mass of unsuitable ones (nightmares and lawsuits).

Know what you're looking for and don't compro- mise.

The Guru Moment

A great way to distinguish yourself as unique in peoples minds is by how you respond in various situations.

As someone whom people wish to be around there should be only two things that **always** surprise you:

> 1) A genuine and sincere act of kindness or any behavior that you like from the prospect

> 2) Your prospects inability to live up to the ideal you are presenting

Understanding this concept makes operant conditioning a meme within your mind control system. What that means in simpler terms is that good responses are naturally rewarded and unwanted responses are naturally denied any reward.

On the one hand when s/he behaves living up to your ideal surprise, not reward, should be emphasized because s/he will respond more to your surprise than to you rewarding him/her. The real reward is your happiness and your acknowledgment of what s/he did. Thus creating a "Good Thing". You can let him/her know it's a "Good Thing" by telling him/her s/he is ready to learn something that few people really understand. This creates a "guru moment" for you in his/her mind.

When the prospect does not live up to the ideal you are presenting it is up to you to point it out with equal surprise and **very** mild disdain creating a "Bad Thing". A mere shaking of the head or a period of isolation from you or your teachings may be enough. If an apology is offered for the misstep your response is that you knew that she would respond the way s/he did so s/he was simply being herself, therefore no apology is needed and treat them like the prodigal son.

In other words you are showing acceptance while letting her know that she can still continue to change.

Many people are not raised with this degree of acceptance and this can create confusion so you must offer something QUICKLY for them to pay attention to, a new teaching, perhaps a metaphor, hypnosis exercise or learning experience. This to will create a "guru moment" but now it is because of a "Bad Thing".

Thus, anytime you respond to your prospect with surprise (whether a Good Thing or a Bad Thing) you can follow it up with a guru-moment. The result is that very quickly your prospect is finding reward in your happiness a "Good Thing" and an eagerness to explore the possibilities of change when they have treaded onto a "Bad Thing".

The ultimate goal of every guru moment is to suspend judgment.

Suspending judgment means being willing to learn.

Learning equals reward.

Judgment equals silence and confusion.

On an occasion when the prospect is not living up to the "Doctrine" and judging instead of learning you can point out the behavior in a very calm tone as if ordering from a menu.

Here is an example of what you could do and say:

"You want to learn how to enjoy life in every moment (the ideal) yet when I left a message you didn't return my call like you had promised." (look off into space confused, not asking for an explanation) "Would you like to experience something important about connection/peace-of-mind/(some value)?"

Take a piece of paper and hold it up with two hands. Tell the prospect to look at it and become connected to it. Wait a few moments and then tear the paper.

"This is what happens to the self when one does not live up to their own expectations. They become torn and it's just as shocking only we try to hide it behind excuses."

Thus you create a guru moment.

10 Ways to Build a Cult-Like Following

Recently I was contacted by a very successful Internet marketer who asked me what I would suggest to someone who wanted to create a cult-like following.

This is right down my ally so I gave him some very good advice that he couldn't wait to put into action but the question got me thinking. What steps are there for anyone who wants people to want his/her attention and wisdom?

The result are 10 ways to build a cult-like following. Of course each one of them could be a book in itself but here goes.

1. Instruction vs. Initiation

There is a marked difference between learning by instruction and learning by initiation.

Most people give instruction. This is nothing more than stating facts and teach processes. Any good teacher does that as well as most bad ones.

Learning by initiation is about creating an experience that makes the learning personal and visceral to the student. A good example of that is the 1984 movie "The Karate Kid" . On the one hand you have the macho western karate instructor who taught his students by instruction in a skill 'n' drill process. On the other hand you have the character played by Pat Marito who says that he will teach Ralph Macchios' character karate in exchange for doing chores. But the chores must be done in a certain way "This way wax on. This way wax off." Only later does the young hero find out that there was a method to his instructors madness and when he figured it out it made complete sense to him as if struck by a lightening bolt.

There are many things that you could simply tell someone and they would intellectually understand but they wouldn't "get it" as an insight. They would only see it as information. The result is that they may use it or they may not.

Teaching by initiation means holding back on simply telling what the student wants to know and instead provide an experience where the student "gets it" on their own.

The subjective experience of the student is that the lesson is much more valuable because 1) they had to work for it and 2) it is felt more personally.

As an example consider your teaching children to climb a rope. You can tell them "Don't slide down the rope because you'll burn your hand." Some will understand some won't. But those who do slide down the rope **will** understand! That's the difference between instruction and initiation. Those who slid down the rope were personally initiated into the under-standing.

2. Being Accessible

Someone once told me that "There are no long lines for the guru at the bottom of the hill."
Making yourself scarce adds perceived value but it also distances you from the masses. If you want a cult-like following you need access to the masses otherwise you're just an ivory tower wannabe.

There is an ingenious compromise.

Be accessible as a person but present your knowl-edge and wisdom as being rare, expensive, mysteri-ous, and only for those who are truly ready for it.

This compromise allows you to build deep personal bonds with people yet have them want more of your presence... as well as be willing to pay for it.

Keep in mind that one cult leader, 2000 years ago, would speak to anyone who would listen but he granted his most sacred attention to his 12 closest disciples.

You can add to this compromise by having "special times" when you are not accessible to anyone. You can tell people that you are meditating, or doing your "spiritual practice" but you don't have to say anything. It's the mystery of **why** you are absent that you want to cultivate.

3. Imply Secret Knowledge

The role of simply remaining calm and silent will recur again in this essay so I can't understate it. Here is where silence is worth a 1000 words. Saying things like "Hmmm... There are 100 possible solutions to that within your own mind." and nothing else implies things that you know and that they should know.

4. Remaining calm as if all-knowing

Any sharp change in your emotional state, with the exception of joy and laughter, should be minimized. Any leader/teacher who goes on an angry rant is demonstrating their own lack of control. If you truly have control it should be demonstrated by an unshakable calm as if everything is happening just as you knew it would.

As an exercise to gain this degree of calm you can use the NLP swish pattern. Here are a simple version of it.

Step 1 – Remember the last time you lost you calm. Revivify it as if you were seeing what you saw at that moment feeling the feeling. Note the image you have in your mind.

Step 2 – Make a second picture of yourself in your mind this one is an image of you calm and poised.

Step 3 – The swish. Quickly go from the first image to the second making sure you pause and interrupt the process before you do it again.

Repeat the steps again.

You'll know you're doing this right when you immediately find yourself switching from the first image to the second without having to practice. You should also notice a rapid calm coming over you when you think about what used to disturb you.

I've always remembered that the scariest martial artist are the ones that don't talk or threaten... they calmly do what they have to do and walk away.

5. Create a detached involvement as if "you" are in a "higher place"

In doing this people will look to you as if there is something more to you than your mere physical presence.

6. Connect deeply with the individual

Here rapport is vital. When you are with people you need to put aside all of your distractions, obligations and problems to focus completely on the person or people you to whom you are speaking.

7. "Chunk Up" whenever possible

This may be a bit abstract to grasp but it's important to creating an appeal because it forces people to think in bigger terms. When you do it consistently it gives the impression that you are always thinking bigger than them.

"Chunking Up" is an NLP term that means referring to something that contains what is spoken about as a subset . It can also refer to something that controls or has a larger reach than the topic at hand.

As an example when a person asks "Do you enjoy adult beverages?" a chunked up response would be "There are many adult pleasures I enjoy." Here, "beverages" is a subset of "pleasures".

Another example : Statement: "I'll go with you if you promise to control yourself." Response "I have no intention of controlling how much I enjoy myself." Here "control" is a subset of "Enjoyment".

8. Always allude to the mysterious

This can be done by doing the opposite of name dropping. Refer to a very skilled person you learned from who doesn't normally take students. Mention an arcane text that describes a mysterious process you went through. Mention it took you ten years of study to read between the lines and find the **real** meaning to the work. You can do that by encouraging someone to keep studying a text they've mentioned and they **will** discover even more.

9. God-Like Confidence

The God Complex is a great example of "chunking up" because it's about seeing EVERYTHING that can possibly happen as if it's all part of the plan and being okay with it.

The God Complex is about having such a larger view of the world and your place in it so that what you are doing, this very moment , regardless of what transpires will be as if it was meant to you be.

The bottom line is that people are going to judge and criticize you; you'll have deal with money and security issues; relationships will change... no matter what. The God Complex includes all of that in a philosophy that allows you to deal with it in a healthy perspective.

10. Appeal to peoples needs and wants

A deep understanding about what people truly respond to is vital if you want to influence anyone. Each individual has their own wants and needs that you have keep in the forefront of your mind.

Good NLP training will help you with that.

People will also respond to the same basic needs being fulfilled; the need to be needed, the need for hope in a tough time, the need to feel in control, the need blame something else for their troubles, the need to learn about something they don't know or not supposed to know.

Conclusion

The desire for a cult-like following has many benefits and many responsibilities. The hardest of the responsibilities is simply living up to what you are presenting to people. For that reason I always recommend that you live what you teach.

The
Perfected Mind Control
Processes

The PMC Processes

"It's dangerous to understand new things too quickly."
~Josiah Warren – **True Civilization**

I hope you haven't jumped to this section without reading everything that has preceded it.

If you have you're not ready. Go back. Start at the beginning and try, really try, to get an idea of this is all about because what follows is what you as an operator will be using with your subject.

If you do it right, everyone you work with will love you. If you do it wrong... you'll pay for it in the long run.

The lesson is (yes, I'll say it again) ***do these processes on yourself first!*** Only then can you use them with the respect they deserve.

Back in the day of the governments MKULTRA project there were plenty of projects to control the thoughts and minds of others. It was after all the height of the cold war and we were running paranoid to forestall nuclear annihilation.

Of all the projects, LSD, brain implants, electro

shock therapy and sensory deprivation the one thing that did show promise was the good old tool of hypnosis.

The goal of these black ops hypnosis experiments was to create a "sleeper" agent that would be hidden behind a barrier of amnesia and when needed the agent could be triggered to carry out a mission and once completed all memories would be hidden again behind the amnesia.

It's very shocking and it's possible so I hope you can understand the gravity of this little project.

The goal of **Perfected Mind Control** is to use this power to help people become more flexible to enjoy life and eventually integrate all the individual identities back into a happier more fun loving person. In the mean time you can also create a wonderful life for yourself with the best friends you can imagine.

Use it wrongly and things will not go so well.

Let me preface this with a news article that came out of Japan:

Dream Incantation Attracts Harem

By Leo Lewis, Times Online

An aging and unprepossesing Tokyo fortune teller who kept a harem of ten women in their twenties for years may have used hypnosis to hold them in his thrall.

Police searching the three-storey home where Hirohito Shibuya, 57, kept the women say that they discovered "how-to" guides on group hypnosis and believe that he used other mind-control techniques under the guise of fortune telling.

Mr Shibuya, who was arrested last week on suspicion of threatening to turn one of his harem members into mincemeat if she left, went to extraordinary lengths to avoid breaching polygamy laws.

Japanese records show that he was married twelve times to ten women between 1999 and August 2004. He divorced one woman and married another in the same day eight times.

"Although it's illegal in Japan, I'm virtually a polygamist," he said. "I contacted my ward office, and officials there said it was not illegal to repeatedly marry and divorce, although they did say it was unprecedented."

Mr Shibuya somehow managed to keep all his former wives under the same roof. He said that they all worked in shops while he stayed at home avoiding strenuous work because of a heart condition.

Although psychologists say it is possible that Mr Shibuya used hypnosis to secure his harem's loyalty, he claims that he learnt in a dream of a magic "love charm". He has refused to share it with the world, but says that "if you chant it, even unattractive men find themselves popular with women".

With that as a Times News article begin to set your mind in the direction of what you think is possible.

If you read this and follow the processes you may find that your initial interest was nothing more than adolescent fantasy for sex, power and control. If so, you are likely to find trouble.

It will only take a few times of having your subjects pounding on your door in the middle of the night and stalking you for your attention to realize how you've gone too far too fast.

Remember that **patience** is your friend and ally and you can use that patience by simply understanding that at some point in your interactions with your prospects that you can start to talk about your understanding about how the mind works. When that opportunity arises don't rush into it... instead treat it like a secret you are not certain you should be revealing because you are not sure your prospect is really ready to hear and learn from it.

A good example of a conversation starter that will lead you to talking about the mind (and eventually to the **PMC** processes) is "There are a lot of interesting things one can learn about the mind. No one ever gave us an instruction manual about it. There are a few things that I don't think most people ever consider..." From there you can talk about how we all want choice but are locked up in habits that limit our choices of response the things.

As you patiently dole out how the mind works and how people easily create their own suffering you should always be demonstrating what you're talking about. In other words, walk your talk and take responsibility for any crap you having in your life.

So far everything you've done is setting the stage for finding a prospect, recruiting them and introducing them to the **PMC** Processes. When they have successfully gone through all the processes they will be official initiates into **PMC**.

Using the **PMC** Processes are the keys that unlock the doors to mind control in both narrow (controlling others thoughts) and broad senses (controlling our own thoughts).

As mentioned at the very beginning of this book the only way to truly understand the power of these processes is to do them on yourself. It will create a level of respect for them as you recite them to your subjects and you may discover that this is not truly what you are cut out to do. If so, great, you've learned a lot. You know what's possible and you can enjoy life hopefully now on your own terms.

Each process is written as a script that should be read to the subject and followed as written. Only after reading the processes aloud many times will you begin to understand what they truly are designed to accomplish.

Unless mentioned, each process should be done one-on-one, not in a group setting. The only exceptions to this rule are 1) when it's so specified and 2) If you are doing them for a group that has already been initiated through the **PMC** processes.

As you lead in to the process you should let your subject understand that what they are going to learn about themselves can be appreciated by only a rare few, and that you are inviting them because you believe they are ready.

Ask your subject to close their eyes, get comfortable and follow each word and meaning.

Your voice needs to be smooth and fluid which can only be achieved by practicing reading each process **aloud** and getting very comfortable with them. Remember the importance of your conviction. Your conviction will empower what you read to be believable.

You will notice that some words in the script are in **bold**. These words are to be emphasized by a brief pause, saying the word/phrase in a lower voice as if giving an order and pausing again briefly before reading on. Exaggerate it if you like.

Please notice that one word you have not read so far is the word "hypnosis". Whether you or anyone else thinks this is hypnosis is of no concern and you can answer that however you see fit.

When I first wrote this as an ebook (I hate ebooks, by the way) I never mention the word "hypnosis" so it's a good time to mention it here.

A lot can be said about hypnosis and I deeply encourage you to do as much hypnosis as possible on yourself and others to get the feeling of it. You'll always find something new, interesting and entertaining when you study and practice it, whether you're doing it on yourself of someone else.

But this is not a hypnosis book, even though it plays a central role. So go ahead and read this book

and others on hypnosis but most importantly practice it. That is where the treasures will be found.

While you can read these processes to the subject
the one thing that I've intentionally ignored is what's
called "the hypnotic induction". Why? Because you
can find one in any other hypnosis book.

Many hypnotists use what is called "The progres-
sive relaxation" induction, or what I call "boring your
subject into submission". My opinion on "the pro-
gressive relaxation induction" is that it is for the
meek and fearful hypnotist who fears that they
might be "doing it wrong" and who has little confidence in exerting control and power. It will also tend
to put your subject to sleep and not in "the process
state" as is intended.

There is one induction called "The Elman Induction" which works quite well and you can find a mil-
lion versions of it on the Internet.

On another note, you've probably have heard it
enough "Do the Processes on yourself!" and a few
people have asked me how to do that.

Keep in mind the whole idea is to learn flexibility
so while you may **think** you have to have someone
read you the processes and "hypnotize" you, anyone
it's just as easy to read the **PMC Processes** and
imagine that you are accepting everything is true for
you.

You can do it so trust yourself.

Good Luck.

"Creating An Inner Voice" PMC Open Process

The purpose of an "open" process is that it can be inserted at anytime during the other **PMC** processes. It's also a very benevolent process that can get anyone to easily feel good about who they are what you're doing with them. In the hypnosis world it does what is called "ego strengthening" for the subject.

For that reason it's quite good at being used for either the subjects first introduction to the **PMC** processes or at anytime as an for example inserting it between other processes.

Additionally, if the operator feels that the subject is not responding well or quickly enough then, no need to rush, simply introduce this simple and enjoyable process that has benefits far beyond the work of **PMC**.

Objectives of the PMC Open Process:

- To build the subjects sense of comfort with the **PMC** processes in general.

- To build the subject confidence in themselves and with the **PMC** processes.

- To build an enjoyable anticipation to learning about themselves and changing to fit their wants and needs.

- To create an ongoing internal voice that will continue to provide positive and beneficial reinforcement to the subject on both a conscious and unconscious level.

• то covertly install the operators voice as a nurturing voice within the subjects consciousness.

Please note as you read this that the suggestions given would be suggestions that we all would like to hear. If these suggestions are an internal endless loop within our minds then we would each be much more likely to feel good about things, be more flexible to challenges, and be happy in general.

For the purpose of anyone new to hypnosis I'm am including the hypnotic induction in hopes that this will make things simpler. Those who are familiar with hypnotic inductions will notice that it is a variation of the famous "Elman" induction.

You'll also notice that early on in the PMC processes the the subject is being enlisted to not merely lay passively with eyes closed but to engage in responses to the operator. For the purpose of PMC this cannot be underestimated.

Responsiveness Is Important!

The PMC Induction
You'll find that this only takes a very short amount of time for you... so ...

Take that moment and close your eyes... begin to become aware of the muscles of your forehead and let them ... **relax**... as the muscles of the forehead relaxes you can notice that the eyes and eye lids naturally... **remain closed**... so now focus on the eyes and eyelids and relax them even further and they will continue to ... **stay closed** ... let your eyes gently gaze now, beneath closed eyelids at the center of your forehead and in a voice within **your mind** tell the eyelids to... **"Stay closed!"**. .. and if you like very briefly test them and stop and **go deeper...** which only means to **become more comfortable...** and you don't even have to move to do that. (PAUSE) ... once again tell the eyelids **"Stay closed"** and if you like briefly test them and stop testing and... **go deeper...** even more relaxed. More comfortable than you were even just a moment ago... and as you notice your degree of relaxation there are even greater levels of relaxation which I call levels A, B and C and let me describe them to you before you actually **go there.**

When you go to Level A ... but don't go there yet ... you'll relax yourself even more than you are right now. And when you reach level A you'll easily be able to move the index finger of the right hand.

When you go to level B I want you to relax so much that it takes all your effort to move the index finger of the right hand... and you may only get just a small visible twitch because you're so relaxed.

Finally, when you go to level C I want you to imagine as if you've relaxed it **all** away so that even though you know that you're trying to move the index finger everything will ... **stay perfectly still.**

So when you're ready go to that level A. When you feel you are more relaxed than you were just a moment ago gently move the index finger of your right hand. (wait) Good!

When you're ready relax even further... go to that level B... where you are so relaxed it takes all your will and effort to move the index finger... because you're so relaxed... you may only get a small motion or twitch enough for me to see. And even thought it's hard I know you can do it. (wait) Good!

Keep relaxing. **Go Deeper...** as if you have relaxed **everything away**... so relaxed that even though you know that you're trying to move the finger... everything stays... perfectly still. .. and you know you're safe. You're completely in control. And if something truly needed your attention you could easily emerge from this state... but now ... even though you know that you're trying to move the finger... everything stays... **perfectly still.**

From here there are four things that we can do whenever you're within this process state . The first is you can simply follow the suggestions and just by doing that you have already achieved a comfortably pleasant state of awareness. You've done very well.

The second thing we can do is I can ask you to imagine something and it can instantly come to mind. For example I'd like you to now imagine a crystal ball with a beautiful red rose inside of it.

The third thing is that I can mention feelings and you can become instantly aware of them. And because you are within this process state now you can notice how easy it is. From now on you don't even have to try your mind will **notice this automatically.** For example even though you might not have been aware of it a moment ago because you are in this pleasant state you can automatically become aware of the shoes on your feet. You might notice the feel or the weight on comfort of discomfort. And even though you haven't been thinking about it you can notice the feeling of your hands resting comfortably where they are right now. You may notice the pressure or texture or the temperature. And you can also notice the feeling of the surface beneath you giving you complete support enough to **relax even more comfortably** with every word.

The forth thing we can do is I can ask you to recall memories and they can instantly come to you. I will ask you to remember only pleasant memories. When you recall these pleasant memories I'd like you let me know by moving the right index finger. (wait) Good!

And now I'd like you to recall a pleasant memory of you around a swing. It could be your swing or the a friends swing or swing at a park or play ground. When that pleasant memory comes to mind move your right index finger. (wait) Good!

And I'd like to remember a time when you learned something of great importance, perhaps even the very first time you learn what it was like to learn. You could have been with a group of people or with someone older and when that pleasant memory comes to mind move your right index finger. (wait) Good! It is times like that when we learn... when everything seems right, if sounds good and it feels real, that it's **like this voice**... that is guiding us. A voice of support, a voice of wisdom, a voice of encouragement. I have a voice like that.... and when you listen for what you **want to learn** you can **hear this voice**. This is your voice. And if you listen... if you truly listen you can **hear this voice** this voice speaking to you right from the center of who you are. Listen.... listen ... and when you **hear this voice** ... move your right index finger. (wait) Good! This is your voice and you can always rely on it ... to give you what you **want to know** ... that will help you... that will guide you ... **that feels good.**

Listen. Listen... and just let this voice repeat and repeat ... right now ... out loud ... to yourself... inside... all that you want to know ...**thats good**... about yourself.

(End of induction)

You have a very strong mind and you **like learning about yourself**... to **find new ways** that will allow you to **make changes ... that you want** which will feel good for you... and it doesn't even matter if you know exactly what those changes are ... it's only important that you **learn and enjoy** as this process naturally takes place... at the deepest level... you realize that there is a part of you that can make changes... wonderful powerful changes... in any area of your life ...because you have throughout your life always made changes ... even now... you're not the same person you were a year ago... or ten years ago... because you've learned ... many things since then... and you realize that there is much more for you that is possible.

Even as you imagine how you wish to **feel more fulfilled** with who you are as you **see yourself at a future time** clearly in your mind... you've already made those changes... being more open to learn... **you have a strong mind..** and **your mind** is now ready to listen to this voice... your voice... reminding you of all the wonderful things you're learning... **that feels good.**

You understand that to make any change you can... **make that change happen**... just like you wanted... and you can also... **allow that change to happen**... naturally, easily...as if it were the simplest thing in the world to do... all you have to do is **be open**... to that change... and **put aside your doubts**... **put aside your hesitations**... and **give yourself permission** ... that will naturally allow you to **feel good about this process**... and all the other wonderful work you are doing right here, right now... at the deepest level of your mind... even though you don't know it ... there is a part of you that is helping you... because you are right here, right now listen to this voice... your voice... telling you just what you need... **that you want** ... it reassures you to ... **just relax** and let it happen. You don't even have to try. All you need to do is listen and let the kind words echo again and again inside **your mind**...and you can naturally... **find resources...** that you didn't even know you had...because they are there... just waiting... waiting ... to **help yourself go deeper** into that pleasant state where this voice is now natural for you to ... **just follow along**... so that during your day... whether you're alone or with people ... on the phone ... or working here... in this way... or even in the quiet moments ... all you have to do is listen... and this voice reminds you... **you're doing fine... relax... just let it happen...go deeper... forget... trust...** your inner mind to do it's perfect work... and reassures you with all the kind words ... That you're hearing... every time you ... **just listen ...** as each word passes over you like a gentle breeze coming from that place inside where you keep everything that you know is true... and during your day... anytime...

when you want to... **feel this well...** all you need to do is ... **close your eyes... and remember** ... the sound of each reassuring word... **that's always there...** giving you the encouragement you want and need.

You give yourself full permission to **feel good** for no reason. So just take some time to recognize the pleasant feelings that you've felt...at any time in your life... **Now...** these feeling are there... as a way to remind you... **you are okay...** and everyday you are doing the best you can ...sometimes under demand-ing circumstances... That is the definition of a hero... You are a good person... you have a strong mind... that can tell the difference between this voice and the the other things you've heard yourself say.

It's true that at times we tell ourselves other things ... that are nothing more than what other people have told us about who they think we are... or who they want us to be... or what you say to yourself when you're frustrated... you can always tell what these voices are because they don't fully reas-sure us... in just the way that we want... so you can always recognize them at times that you're feeling bad and down on yourself... and just let them fade away... these voices don't really matter... you don't even have to think about them... their not even im-portant... as you turn your attention to your own voice.. this voice... that completely reassures you... in all the ways... that you want.

Take a moment now you create at some level of mind... a mechanism... an endless loop of wonderful feelings, suggestions and encouragement that you're hearing by this very positive and supportive internal voice...that reminds you you are loved and supported by everything around you... knowing that all you have to do is **be**... exactly who you are... and that you are not your thoughts... thoughts are just what you tell yourself ... you are not your feelings... you are something greater... you are at the deepest level something wonderful ... and all of this is true simply because you were born ... a child ... to human parents... no matter where you go... no matter what happens around you ... there is a part of you that always knows you are a loved and perfect so that when you want to learn more about yourself and make a change... you can learn easily and with pleasure and that change can happen just the way you want... and every part of you can **make this change easy**... go ahead ... **go deeper**... and enjoy the process ...that's taking place right here... right now... as this voice... your voice ... just flows and gives all the kind words you need to **remember you're okay**... and you can feel a strength and loving energy at any time of the world around you loves you and supports you... and you don't have to do a thing... just permit it... allow it all to take place... just as you wanted.. just as you needed ...when you first came to hear this voice. ...

You see yourself standing tall, relaxed, feeling at ease and able... to accomplish each of the goals you set out to accomplish... naturally, easily as if it were the simplest thing in the world to do... you don't even have to give it a second thought.

You hear within your own mind the power of a strong internal voice...**that's always there**... putting you at ease.. and you **feel it's encouragement** ... as each word and sound support as you... to do what you need to do... this is your voice... There is always something wonderful about being who you are.

Within each sound... **that you're hearing**... now and as you listen to your inner voice... there is a comfort... **that you enjoy**... learning more and more about yourself... by just following along ... and you can **welcome that comfort** ... in... deeper and deeper... so no matter where you are... you can **feel at ease**... and know that you have all the resources you need to accomplish what you want... you focus in on your what is important and you act on it naturally and easily just as you wanted to...

Go Deeper... forget... trust your inner mind to do it's perfect work.

So that even in your dreams this voice.. your voice... can be there as a gentle guide so perhaps tonight and tomorrow too... you can begin to create a dream that will be coming together to create new possibilities... of how good you can feel about yourself ... just by learning more about who you are... and your willingness to find out more...

You give yourself full permission to **feel good** for no reason. So just take some time to recognize the pleasant feelings that you've felt...at any time in your life... **Now**... these feeling are there... as a way to remind you... **you are okay**... And you don't even have to think... about it... you don't even have to remember that... **it's there**... repeating in the back of your mind... like a constant pleasant reminder that... **you're okay** ... no matter what... It just makes you able to **feel good** that at anytime all you have to do is **just listen**...at the deepest level... It's reminding you **you're a good person**... **that feels good**... no matter where you are... it's like someone you can trust is ready to give you support and encouragement... and this person is always with you... you can enjoy anything fully... at any time... and you enjoy learning about yourself... and how you can change to suit whatever is happening ... whether alone or with people, on the phone, or just relaxing ... **like what you're doing right now.**

So all you have to do is just relax... **go deeper**... beyond any thought or memory because you don't have to even think... about it... create an opening and welcome in this pleasant voice... and wrap yourself around it... tighter than you've ever wrapped yourself around anything before you realize it... it creates a gentle current of pleasure **that goes deeper**... and deeper ... inside you... there is a feeling that something wonderful is about to happen... as this comfort and pleasure builds and the words wash over you like a gentle breeze... **Something wonderful is about to happen** ... and you can **now** move through the world with a sense of calm anticipation... not knowing exactly what wonderful thing you'll soon discover about yourself... and how you can enjoy things more, and more.. and more... intensely... letting this voice continue ... to encourage you to do what you want most to do... **you have the strength**... and all the resources you are just waiting for you to call upon them... **NOW.**

And even though this only took a brief minute of time you'll be amazed and surprised at how well you've done. But time doesn't even matter because of how you **feel so good** about this new feeling of control **that you feel.**

As you gently bring your awareness back begin to

Perfected Mind Control – www.MindControl101.com

become aware that even in the silence that is around you... you can still **feel wonderful**... that this voice is there with you.

And if you're listening to this just prior to sleep you can easily turn off the recording and drift into a deep and restful dream ... filled **sleep.** At any other time you can find you energy returning fully aware awake and feeling wonderful. On the count of three allow your eyes to open as bring yourself fully back and aware of the environment around you.

One... You give yourself full permission to **feel good** for no reason. So just take some time to recognize the pleasant feelings that you've felt...at any time in your life... **Now**... these feeling are there... as a way to remind you... **you are okay**...this voice will always be there as you begin to return more and more aware of my voice, the comfort of your body. Bring the energy of awareness more fully back.

Two... everything is in it's proper place as you become more and more aware awake, alert and feeling wonderful.

Three ... Take a deep breath **now! Inhale deeply**... Let your arms stretch. Let your eyes open... refreshed alert WIDE AWAKE... feeling great. OPEN YOUR EYES.

PMC Process #1
"The Importance of the Process State"

Objectives:

•   Have the subject understand the context of "mind control" which is to gain more flexibil- ity in their thoughts and behaviors.

•   Create "The Process State" that the sub- ject will look forward to. Within this "Process State" changes can be made.

•   Have the subject gain control of the abil- ity to create an internal sense of comfort and pleasure.

•   Frame the words "Deep" and "Deeper" to mean "more comfort and more pleasure".

•   To test the subjects ability to create am- nesia, further demonstrating control that **they** have over their thoughts.

• Create an experience that is pleasant for the subject and a feeling of anticipation for other processes.

• Responsiveness, the ability to respond comfortably and automatically to questions and suggestions, is established as a key to pleasure and enjoyment. If this is not demonstrated consistently by the end of the process session the subject repeats **PMC** Process #1 for next session.

This will only take an instant of your time to experience. The purpose of this process is to gain a clear and full understanding of how the mind works... sometime it works for us... and sometimes it works against us.. and understanding the workings of the mind you can gain control of mental processes so that life can be more enjoyable, you can **have more pleasure** and **feel completely free** from hurts worries and irritations that **your mind** can bring up by habit.

You'll learn this and **get a good feeling** for it through creating a state of learning that is called the process state that's comfortable, flexible, quick to learn, **that feels good** whenever you enter the process state you'll discover new things about yourself, **your mind** and how you can **create joy and pleasure** at will.

Each time you listen to this process from beginning to end you'll feel more comfort and ease, you'll return rested and energized feeling wonderful about yourself and your experience and learned about yourself.

Learning in the process state is not achieved by studying or by awareness of your external environment but by being able to **go deeply inside** to review, learn and **experience** what it is that's just waiting for you to be discover.

Within the process state comfort is important and a person can **feel comfort** first by simply being aware of your physical body and relaxing... **Get comfortable... now**... as your comfort grows more and more pleasant it's important that you understand that during each process you will hear the word "deeper" and all that word "deeper" is to mean is to **increase your comfort**... which will demonstrate to you by experience that you are gaining more and more control of your thoughts and **your mind.** So **begin now** to notice your body and take a few moments to **create comfort** for yourself. (pause) and as you hear the word "deeper" **increase that comfort** in what ever way is most natural and easy for you. (pause) Now **go deeper** (pause) and as you **experience more comfort** acknowledged that to yourself that you are gaining more control (pause) now **go deeper** again creating even more comfort so that each time through each process you experience a more pleasant and enjoyable sense of comfort **and trust** the process that is taking place even as you might begin to notice that on occasion **your mind** might wander which is perfectly natural and you can allow your mind to wander as you respond fully to each suggestion and to each suggestion you can **go deeper** (pause) **create more comfort** and enjoyment which is a natural part of the process state. Each time you **go deeper** you can consciously acknowledge the control that you are experiencing over your thoughts, your emotions, your body and **your mind**.

An important part of the learning in the process state is that of easily being able to respond in simple and pleasant ways to each suggestion such as responding to the word "**deeper**" by **feeling very comfortable right now** or you'll notice that if a questioned is asked you **easily respond** with

Perfected Mind Control – www.MindControl101.com

movement of your head or a simple word "yes" or "no" and in so doing you are learning even greater control to **build that sense of comfort** in any situation, any time, and under any circumstance your ability to **feel comfort** is there as a resource for you rely on.

So, now **go deeper**, so that each word that you hear more easily begins to create it's own smooth and pleasant place – all your objections behind you – that feels natural and easy so that you are now learning more and more about yourself.

And because responding to suggestions is vital to learning in the process state **go deeper now** and when you feel the deeper sense of comfort easily nod your head or say "yes" (wait for response). Good! And each time you **respond fully** in such a way you **open yourself** to learn more... so now again **go deeper** and when you have, again nod your head or say "yes" (wait for response) Good! And will you continue to do so with each suggestion? (wait for response) Good! **Go deeper** knowing that each time you **respond fully** you will learn more and more about yourself, your world, **your mind** and gain greater and greater control.

And so you're ready to learn.

Within the mind there are many places and each place within your mind has an important role in learning. There is a place where you put things that you know are true. Things like the sun rises each morning or perhaps it's true that you feel a wonderful feeling towards someone very close to you. Take a moment and find or create that place where things are true and when you have it simply respond with a nod or say yes. (pause) Good. Now **go deeper** and continue to respond pleasantly in just that manner. In this place where things are true you can begin to accept each pleasant change you are making as true and real for you. Each new wonderful thing that you learn about yourself can now become true because you place it right there where things are true. Take a moment to make all this true and when you are done nod your head or say "yes". (pause) Good. **Go deeper.**

With each new thing that you learn you will know it's true... now you can **make each suggestion true...that you like**... by simply allowing it to naturally fit, so comfortably into the place where things are true. So now, on a **deeper** level suggest to your **deeper** inner mind to **make that happen**... and once you have nod your head or say "yes" and allow yourself to **go deeper.** (pause)

Good. **Go deeper...** forget.... trust... your inner mind to do it's perfect work and make all that you experience here today real, right, and true for you. And so it is.

There is another place within **your mind** that you'll find quiet useful. A place far behind you where you put things that are no longer true for you and things that no longer really matter... things like you used to live in another town but now you don't, or that you used to ride a different vehicle but now you don't. Find or create that place inside **your mind now** and when you have nod your head or say yes (pause) Good. This is the place where things no longer matter and in this place you can put all your

Perfected Mind Control – www.MindControl101.com

worries, all your hesitations, all your excuses and all the things that used to hold you back. Because it's so pleasant you can now let those things begin to slide or fall back there where you don't even have to think about them. They don't even really matter. As you **let that happen now** and notice it simply nod your head or say "yes" and then **go deeper.** (pause) Good.

And even further back in that place that no longer matters is all of your forgettings, all the names of people you've met just once...lost to time. All the phone numbers ... forgotten... filled with unimportant things piled **deep** and unknown... So that you can have even greater control of your mind take moment now and find that place of forgettings and you have it nod your head or say 'yes' and **go deeper** (pause)

So that you can learn even more about yourself I'd like to demonstrate the power you truly have over **your mind**... just for the even the briefest moment, in that place of forgetting, right now **put your name right there**, you might find it confusing but you **realize you're fine**, and when you've done that nod your head or say 'yes' and congratulate yourself on learning the power of control. (pause) Good. Now retrieve your name. Do you have it? (pause) Good. **Go deeper...** Forget... trust your **deeper** inner mind to do it's perfect work to follow each pleasant suggestion **that you like** to lead you to greater knowledge and understanding.

Now, I'm going to reveal to you a secret that prevents so many people from really learning how to enjoy life. The reason is that of judgment. We've all felt the pain of not being understood. We've all felt what it was like to have someone reject us without ever considering what we're experiencing and feeling and in the same way by us judging we ourselves loose out on truly understanding what's possible...that can make all the difference. Before anyone can learn what it is they truly want to know, you have to experience it as real... to find the real joy, pleasure and excitement of life. Can you **see that as true?** (pause).

Good. So while you're learning through this process put all your judgment aside...**go deeper**... forget... and allow yourself to simply let go and let each word wash over you as if it were your own thoughts guiding you to **deeper** understandings more about yourself.

At the same time we all know what it's like have someone with your who truly understands your hopes, your fears, your feelings and desires. And to **share that openness** one does that without judging, only accepting, what is true and real for you right now.

(this you can repeat this paragraph at various times throughout the process) and right now...you enjoy learning about yourself and this process of learning. You are strong and in control enough to easily **let go** and **feel pleasure** with each suggestion your mind understands, your body grows strong and you're eager to learn more...and let all your analyzing simply fall away to the place where you put things that no longer matter, it isn't important, it doesn't even matter, you don't even have to think...about it. Just enjoy and accept that you are unique with a **deeper** understanding of what is true

Perfected Mind Control – www.MindControl101.com

and real and important to you there is so much pleasure in letting go and learning in this way as you let each word that you hear becomes part of your own thoughts and repeats, repeats, right now, out loud, to yourself, inside, you have so much more strength, control and confidence in yourself. *(this you can repeat at various times throughout the process)*

It is only through your strength that you can **let go** and allow this learning to take place so easily that it seems like a faint and pleasant dream that fades naturally from your memory upon returning from the process state. Yet you know all of this is true.

And each time you think back to this process all you need to remember is the special feeling of know-ing that you're learning...more and more about your-self ...and that you eagerly look forward to this lis-tening to this process again and again because each time you do you instantly return to that pleasant **deep** learning state called the process state. It feels wonderful and all you have to do is let go, relax and **go deeper.**

Between now and the next process session you will discover more about who you are and new healthy things **that you enjoy**. You look forward to the next session with a calm readiness. Each day for you is special and a each night you will dream won-derful dreams that will be coming together for your greater joy and happiness now each suggestion naturally fits and is real for you. Each suggestion is right there in that part of you where you keep every-thing that is true.

As you look now to that place **that's true** you can tell **it just feels right** to know you're learning in this way you have more energy throughout your day, free from worry and concern. You are changing just as you wanted, just as you needed when you first came to hear this voice. Because inside you there is a voice of confidence security, comfort and strength. This voice is your voice and it guides you revealing new and wonderful things about yourself. Liston ... Liston... as this voice echoes pleasantly at the deepest level of your inner mind whether you are asleep or awake or in this process state of learning as you are right now this voice is your true guide. There is a calm and comfort as it guides you. So that in the quiet moments of your thoughts the pleasant whispers of this voice comforts you and gives you strength. This is your voice and all of this is true.

So just let go. **Go deeper.** Forget... trust... the power of your inner mind and this voice to guide you so you don't even have to remember... that each suggestion is all part of your true self being revealed to you as each wonderful day unfolds before you there is a quiet eagerness to explore what more you can learn about yourself... explore how much more your life is getting better, better and better in every way. You truly are eager to listen to this process every day and find out more about yourself.

You now understand the importance of truly learning in the process state because you can truly test what is real and you know this is true because you are focused, relaxed and feeling absolutely wonderful about what is taking place right this very moment as each word simply washes over you...and you may begin to find that as you focus in on the sound of

Perfected Mind Control – www.MindControl101.com

each word and words of each sound that you don't know if it what you are hearing or your own thoughts and it doesn't even really matter.

Tonight, perhaps tomorrow too, your deeper, inner mind can give you a dream, a very special dream that clarifies the problem indicates the source perhaps, but tells you quite clearly how to solve your concerns and problems now. And each night afterwards, until you understand it, until you decide to do it or not, that dream can return to you in one form or another.

And every day as you go about your business, your unconscious can find something, some thought, perception, awareness, a taste perhaps or a sensation, or even a color, that seems familiar and reminds you of something, reminds you of what your unconscious mind is trying to tell you, until you fully understand and use that understanding for you.

Because you enjoy learning about yourself and this process of learning. You are strong and in control enough to easily **let go.** It is only through your strength that you can **let go** and feel pleasure with each suggestion your mind understands, your body grows strong and you're eager to learn more...and let all your analyzing simply fall away to the place where you put things that no longer matter, it isn't important, it doesn't even matter, you don't even have to think...about it. Just enjoy and accept that you are unique with a deeper understanding of yourself and what is true and real and important to you there is so much pleasure in letting go and learning in this way as you let each word that you hear become part of your own thoughts and repeat, repeat, like a comforting echo, right now, out loud, to your-self, inside, you have so much more strength, control and confidence in yourself. You have a very strong mind. You have a very strong will and it is by the strength of **your mind** and will that each time you listen to this process you will **go deeper** beyond any doubt and hesitation and enjoy the rest it gives you from concern and thought with the understanding that to learn in this process state is to **make real changes...that feels good.**

So as you gently and pleasantly emerge from this process state you will find each time you listen it be-comes easier ... and easier. Each time you **go deeper** and each time you return rested, comfort-able, confident in that you're doing the right thing to improve your life just the way you wanted, just as you needed when you first heard this voice and all you have to remember is that it felt wonderful and that you are changing in all the ways **that you want.**

So as you return from this pleasant process state you will feel rested and alert a wide smile will come to your face as if you were told a special secret about who you truly are eager to listen to this proc-ess every day.

And even though this only took a short **minute** you will be surprised and amazed at how well you've done. Yes, even though you've spent a short minute in this pleasant process state you will be amazed at how well you've done.

And this is so.

So gently you will guide your back from this pleas-ant state returning your awareness to this voice,

Perfected Mind Control – www.MindControl101.com

your breathing, feeling wonderful, alert and rested. At the time your eyes open you will smile widely with a sense of ease remember clearly the joy and pleasure that you now feel so deeply.

(pause)

Take a deep breath and allow the movement to return slowly and comfortably to your body. Eyes open. Alert. Awake. Feeling absolutely wonderful.

[Once the subject has returned from the process state you point out the importance of being able to respond quickly in this state and then practice going in and out of this state on command. Also important to practice this while standing and moving, walking. Once that is accomplished you suggest that as the subject walks closer and closer to their car they will enter this state and gain a new insight or feeling which they will remember and report to you at the next process.]

STOP!!

Do not go any further.

You were warned and I'm warning you again.The goal of each PMC process is to increase flexibility in *you* and the people to whom you present these processes.

There is a huge amount still ahead that many people might begin to become very concerned about.

Let's talk about the psychological term "projection" for a moment.

Projection is the process of seeing something in others that one would deny in themselves. If you think for a moment these processes are about using and abusing the people with whom you them on, you are dead wrong and I highly recommend that you seriously consider what it is that you are afraid of *in yourself* that you might do to someone.

You've been *repeatedly* encouraged to go through these processes yourself to gain some real respect for the power and how to use it effectively.

Perfected Mind Control – www.MindControl101.com

So think of someone that you trust and go first! I dare you!

Okay.

If you think you're ready to keep reading you've been warned.

PMC Process #2
"The Source of Suffering – The Key to Freedom"

Objectives:

• To clearly explain that the reason for all the trouble is the automatic and unconscious judgment.

• To have the subject willingly put aside all judgment to be able to experience whatever is suggested as enjoyable.

• Give suggestions during the process state that will be tested immediately after emerging from the process state.

• Give suggestions that will be carried out later in the absence of the operator during the days that follow and immediately prior to the next **PMC** Process without the coaching of the operator.

• To verify that the subject will out of habit automatically enter the process state when asked.

Test of last process:

Did they listen to the process every day?

During the last process did s/he emerge with a broad smile?

Prior to starting did the subject appear ea-ger/excited to participate in this process?

Did the subject report any new insight or feeling from the last process?

Did the subject report vivid dreams?

Just **like this...** before... will take no time at all... It will take only an instant. The purpose of this proc-ess is to learn more about how the mind naturally works. Sometimes it works for us... to help us **feel comfortable** and to **ease all concerns**... and al-lows us to **go deeper within** to make new discover-ies... sometimes it works against us ... making con-clusions that we find out are wrong... and as you learn about **your mind** you learn more about your-self so that each new experience within the process state... creates joy and allows you to **go deeper...** than the time before .. **that feels comfortable...** simple and easy to learn in this the process state... and you know that each time you hear the words "**go deeper**" you will create more pleasant sense of comfort for your body and ...**your mind...**

So just let everything happen ... exactly as it wants to happen. Don't try to make anything hap-pen...don't try to stop... anything from happening. Just allow everything to please itself and happen as it feels like it wants to, naturally and easily as if it were the simplest thing in the world to do...**go deeper**...and relax so that **your mind** can **let go completely** and experience to trust the process state so that you can learn what it is you need know about yourself and gain more control of your life....

...now you can listen... listen for a voice **that you trust**... inside you is this voice... this voice has a calm comforting presence **that guides you** to make all the changes **that you need**...to enjoy life. This voice is your voice... always there like a friendly guide...and as you listen you can find that the words simply wash over you so smooth soft, like the warm touch of summer breeze you can hear each word guiding you... and even in the quite moments of your thoughts are the gentle whispers of this voice reminding you "You're safe. Relax. Let go and let me guide you." In so doing you can enjoy...whatever you are experiencing right this very moment.

...and so it can seem like a gentle fading dream yet you know that you will respond fully, easily, naturally to each opportunity to learn. And so that you can learn **go deeper** and each time you hear the words "**go deeper**" you will go past all your con-scious thoughts and **create more comfort** for your-self and your body and **your mind**.

And you will respond to every suggestion you hear and each time you respond to each suggestion you hear you will **go deeper** as if it were the most natu-ral thing in the world to do. And each time you are ask to respond to a question you will nod your head or say "yes" and each time you do nod your head or say "yes" you will **go deeper** with more ease. Do you agree? (wait for response) Good! **Go deeper** as your pleasant reward for doing so well.

You have already learned that you can learn any-thing as long as your allow yourself to experience it for yourself as true. This provides you with the greatest freedom and pleasure. The freedom to enjoy ...every moment... just as you are right now... you also have learned that the greatest obstacle to learning, truly learning, is the criticism and judgment of the conscious mind... to know the true limitation that of the judgment I'd like you to search your memory for a time when you criticized without being understood. (pause) do you remember that time? (wait for response) In that moment, as you relive it, it is as if you created a doorway of invitation that opened up ... but instead of the kindness of understanding thrust in is the harsh pain of judgment ...growing more painful and sharp...denying who you are... forcing your to feel it's hurt... and then comes the shame of being judged... pushing it's way deeper within you and burning at that precious part of you....until all you could do is escape... Do you remember? (wait for response) Yes. And so it is that you create the same pain when you judge and evaluate.

You can **let that go now** and **go deeper** and allow those hurts to fall away. **Let go of judging** so that you can truly learn. Because now **you are learning** how the only way to **enjoy every moment** ...**enjoy this moment**... is to **let go of judgment, go deeper** and learn from a new direction.

When you **do that now** you are free... free from hurt, free to experience new things in new ways. This provides you with a sense of meaning and comfort and you can feel that comfort right now, is this true? (response) Good!

Go deeper...forget... trust your deeper inner mind... to do it's perfect work and create more com-

Perfected Mind Control – www.MindControl101.com

fort for yourself, your body and **your mind. Go deeper.** (pause) **go deeper** (pause) **go deeper** because now you are ready to learn how to create true joy.

True joy, true pleasure only comes from acceptance of what is happening. Only then can you yield to the possibilities that are right in front of you and learn.

This can happen simply the moment that you become aware. The moment that you **realize now is the time** and you **focus in deeply** and as you **do that** it's like you **see a door in front you** and you allow that door to **open up** to let that curiosity enter you. That tingling smooth feeling of curiosity penetrating deep within you as an excitement to learn more and as it builds to rich colorful brilliance you discover that feeling of acceptance. Only by accepting can you truly learn. The acceptance guides you to open yourself to it knowing that all **this is right** and as the feeling of acceptance goes deeply inside of you with it's velvety soft warmth it becomes you and you can learn and understand even more about yourself and what is possible so with pleasure you can wrap yourself around this feeling of acceptance so that slowly, gently and in it's own time with each step toward acceptance, taking it in **go deeper**, it begins to build, stronger and stronger until you culminate in understanding and curious to learn more.

And so it is that one returns to curiosity... and you have that curiosity to know more about yourself and create more joy...**go deeper... forget...** trust your **deeper** inner mind to do it's perfect work so all you have to remember is that you enjoy the process state and each time that you listen to your process learning will occur on **deeper** level that ever before...you realize it the whole process is over in an instant and you fell wonderful.

And just listen to your inner voice, **this voice** that comforts and guides you. Each sound of each word gently washes over you like a warm caress of an angels wing so you don't even have to listen and remember you can remember to forget completely as you follow all the suggestions without hesitation or doubt simply washing them away from all your conscious awareness because each word is a natural part of your thoughts and **your mind.** And all of this is true.

True joy, true pleasure only comes from acceptance of what is happening. Only then can you yield to the possibilities that are right in front of you and learn.

This can happen simply the moment that you **become aware**. The moment that you **realize now is the time** and you **focus in deeply** and as you **do that** it's like you **see a door in front you** and you allow that door to **open up** to let that curiosity enter you. That tingling smooth feeling of curiosity penetrating deep within you as an excitement to learn more and as it builds to rich colorful brilliance you discover that feeling of acceptance. Only by accepting can you truly learn. The acceptance guides you to **open yourself** to it knowing that all **this is right** and as the feeling of acceptance goes deeply inside of you with it's velvety soft warmth it becomes you and you can learn and understand even more about yourself and what is possible so, **with pleasure**, you can wrap yourself around this feeling of acceptance so that slowly, gently and in it's own time with each step toward acceptance, taking it in **go deeper**, it begins to build, stronger and stronger until you culminate in understanding and curious to learn more.

And so it is that one returns to curiosity... and you have that curiosity to know more about yourself and create more joy...**go deeper... forget...** trust your **deeper** inner mind to do it's perfect work so all you have to remember is that you enjoy the process state and each time that you listen to your process learning will occur on **deeper** level that ever before.

And all of this is true... and will continue at a deep level of your mind unaware that you'll be pleasantly surprised at what you'll discover without meaning to discover it.

With in **your mind**, there is that powerful place where you put all things you know are true. It is there that **make all this real** without thought, judgment and it feels so right, it feels so natural to learn in this way free from memory as each word slides **deeply** into that place where things are true.

You don't even have to remember ...**all of this is true**... you can forget to remember or remember to forget what it is that you're already allowing yourself to discover on your own ...naturally, easily, and all you have to do is let go and let this voice, your voice, guide you repeating, repeating, right now, out loud to yourself inside is that comforting voice guiding you and you can easily respond without thought or judgment because all of this is true, is it not? ...and just allow your head to nod or say "yes" and go deeper. (wait)

Perfected Mind Control – www.MindControl101.com

and to make this natural, easy, enjoyable and fun let any conscious memory or awareness of each suggestion disappear so you that you can learn effortlessly...let it fall away into the place behind you all your forgettings because remembering doesn't even matter when you learn in this pleasant manner and each time you remember to forget you demonstrate to yourself on a deep level the control you have over **your mind**.

To prove to your deeper inner mind the ease of your learning upon returning form the process state you will begin to laugh uncontrollably and for no apparent reason and free from memory of this suggestion you will find yourself enjoying laughing without control just because it feels right. So as you hear these words echoing within **your mind** your deeper inner mind accept them naturally and easily free from judgment or memory ...gone... forget ... trust your deeper inner mind to carry out each suggestion because you want to learn more and more more about yourself...and upon returning form the process state you will begin to laugh uncontrollably and for no apparent reason and free from memory of this suggestion you will find yourself enjoying laughing without control just because it feels right.

Go deeper...now ... with each time you listen this enjoyable process you will go deeper... deeper and deeper ... each time deeper than the time before... You enjoy listening every day to the process given you so that you can learn about yourself and gain more control of the world around you.

Each day you enter deep into the process state you return rested, energized, alert and enjoying life more. Each day you enter deep into the process state you return rested, energized, alert and enjoying life more.

And this is true...is it not? ...and just allow your head to nod or say "yes" and go deeper. (wait) Good and so it is that your deeper inner mind can now do all the work for you automatically, instantly, so that you don't have work, to try or even to think...all you have to do is let your deeper inner mind hear each word as right for you and you will make it your own thoughts...erasing any memory of the words so that everything you want happens just as you want it and it's a wonderful surprise.

You are surprised at what you are learning and that you have never learned it before in your life is so exciting to discover these new things and new things about you. The excitement follows you each day as you look forward to the next process learning...following you just as this voice follows you because this is your voice and it feels ... just right to learn in this way.

Go deeper...forget trust your deeper inner mind to do it's perfect work and carry out each suggestion without effort and free from thought and even though you have only spent a brief minute with the process state you realize the freedom you are gaining as you learn in this manner. **Go deeper.**

So for now as you **go deeper** allow a part of **your mind** visualize in an easy natural way the mind being rewired, reprogrammed to **experience joy, pleasure** at each suggestion you hear in the process state and because all of this happens without your effort or conscious awareness forget the suggestion completely and let it happen naturally, easily and automatically like it were a pleasant and reassuring habit.

And so that you learn and enjoy and enjoy the learning Over the next few days automatically, free from thought or effort you'll notice yourself relaxing quietly and remembering this voice ... taking a whole moment to yourself... to enjoy the process state... all on your own ... and being completely safe and secure and surprised at how **deep** you go...all the way down... only doing this in times when your daily activities allow it ... without warning while in a safe environment... automatically you find yourself enjoying the process state and being so surprised you have to tell me at our next meeting.

Thats right....so that you learn and enjoy and enjoy the learning Over the next few days automatically, free from thought or effort or memory of these words you'll notice yourself relaxing quietly and remembering this voice ... taking a whole moment to yourself... to enjoy the process state... all on your own ... and being completely safe and secure and surprised at how **deep** you go...all the way down... only doing this in times when your daily activities allow it ... without warning while in a safe environment... automatically you find yourself enjoying the process state and being so surprised you have to tell me at our next meeting.

And your inner mind agrees to this so that you can now nod your head or say 'yes' and this is true, is it not? (wait).

And each time we meet you will be ready to learn

more and go deeper so that your mind is ready to make changes **that will create pleasure** in every level of your life.

And this is true and will be true from this time forward because you are automatically placing each suggestion, each word from this voice, your voice, right there where you put everything **that is true**... and as you **listen from that place where things are true** you will always **hear this voice** guiding you to learn more and make the right changes ...whether you are learning in the process state or fully alert, on the phone or in any setting this voice is there comforting you, supporting you... completely in every area of life.

Because you enjoy learning about yourself and this process of learning. You are strong and in control enough to easily **let go.** It is only through your strength that you can **let go** and feel pleasure with each suggestion your mind understands, your body grows strong and you're eager to learn more...and let all your analyzing simply fall away to the place where you put things that no longer matter, it isn't important, it doesn't even matter, you don't even have to think...about it. Just enjoy and accept that you are unique with a deeper understanding of yourself and what is true and real and important to you there is so much pleasure in letting go and learning in this way as you let each word that you hear become part of your own thoughts and repeat, repeat, like a comforting echo, right now, out loud, to yourself, inside, you have so much more strength, control and confidence in yourself. You have a very strong mind. You have a very strong will and it is by the strength of **your mind** and will that each time you listen to this process you will **go deeper** beyond any doubt and hesitation and enjoy the rest it gives you from concern and thought with the understanding that to learn in this process state is to **make real changes...that feels good.**

Now... inside **your mind** I'd like you create a event that I will vividly describe to you... of a time in the future... Where you can instantly enter the process state just as you are now... so that each time you are ready and **feel anticipation** for entering the process state you **go deeper** and more enjoyably than the time before you know it you are enjoying the process state... as you create this event **inside your mind** naturally easily by simply hearing the words "**go deeper**" you create an opening to allow the process state in and you embrace it tightly... and so it is with each imagining of a future time you clearly see, crisply hear and dramatically feel yourself wrapping yourself around the this wonderful and enjoyable state of mind ...and you are ready to learn.

And so she did imagine that just as she was described... is was all so clear to her... she was there at that moment hearing the words "**go deeper**" and she felt the words pull at her like strong and caring arms... all around her was nothing but this voice... her voice that echoed all her kindest thoughts so it was so easy to follow... so simple to just let go... **deeper and deeper** than the time before... and even after she remembered only wanting waiting and anticipating the next occasion that she could return... It was all so clear to her as she heard the words and felt their warm touch...

That's right you see so clearly that time in the future...any time in the future... where you hear the words "**go deeper**" and feel swiftly returning **deeper** than the time before...

So as you gently and pleasantly emerge from this process state you will find each time you listen it becomes easier ... and easier. Each time you **go deeper** and each time you return rested, comfortable, confident in that you're doing the right thing to improve your life just the way you wanted, just as you needed when you first heard this voice and all you have to remember is that it felt wonderful and that you are changing in all the ways **that you want.**.. and only a moment has past.

So as you return from this pleasant process state you will feel rested and alert a wide smile will come to your face as if you were told a special secret about who you truly are eager to listen to this process every day...and only a moment has past.

And even though this only took a short **minute** you will be surprised and amazed at how well you've done. Yes, even though you've spent a short **minute** in this pleasant process state you will be amazed at how well you've done.

And this is so.

So gently you will guide your back from this pleasant state returning your awareness to this voice, your breathing, feeling wonderful, alert and rested. At the time your eyes open you will smile widely with a sense of ease remember clearly the joy and pleasure that you now feel so deeply.

Perfected Mind Control – www.MindControl101.com

(pause)

Take a deep breath and allow the movement to return slowly and comfortably to your body. Eyes
open. Alert. Awake. Feeling absolutely wonderful.

**[Once the subject has returned from the
process state you point out the importance of
being able to respond quickly in this state and
then practice going in and out of this state on
command. Also important to practice this
standing and moving, walking. Once that is accomplished you suggest that as the subject
walks closer and closer to their car they will
enter this state and gain a new insight or feeling which they will remember and report to you
at the next process.]**

Process #3

"The Power of the Process State"

Objectives:

· Train/test the subject to enter the proc- ess state on the command **"go deeper"**.

· Amnesia on command.

· Test to see if the suggestion given in previous process were successfully carried out. If not **PMC** Process #2 is repeated. No empha- sis is given to failure only on learning flexibility and increased enjoyment.

· ***If all tests are successful suggest New Behavior be performed that is out- side of the subjects norm. The new behav- ior is done w/ great pleasure and carried out w/o the subjects memory of the sug- gestions but the subject will be eager to report it to you.***

· Frame the unconscious mind as the place where creativity, flexibility and enjoyment come from via the "Process State". Get confir- mation and agreement.

· Frame the conscious, thinking mind as the reason they have not experienced deep, profound and consistent joy and pleasure in their life. Get confirmation and agreement. Put aside all conscious awareness to maximize true enjoyment.

• Suggestions of vivid and pleasurable dreams that will eagerly be reported at next process.

Test of last process:

• Did the subject report on automatically entering the process state and not need to be prompted to tell you?

• Did the subject laugh spontaneously upon emerging from the last process?

• Did the subject report a new insight as they walked to their car after the last process?

Go deeper. The purpose of this process is you to learn more about who you are and to explore further .. your response-ability ... to open you up... for beyond question or doubt ... and inside **your mind** you will ... have all the resources.. you need to ... just let go... give yourself permission to ... live freely... from the burdens and conditions of the world... let go ... let completely go... and **go deeper**... **inside your mind**... so that ... you will ... learn to **get the benefits you desire** ... as you let go completely... trusting... that you're in the right place .. at the right time... to give yourself permission to enjoy what is happening ... right this very moment ... free from doubt or hesitation ...

Now **go deeper** and allow your powerful inner

mind to demonstrate to you it's true power that only the inner mind can reveal to you... with this process state you will learn to enjoy more choices and more options because you know that the more choices you have the more free you are in every situation ... and begin to let the old conscious mind full of thoughts and worries just slip away... and drift off... freeing you... completely to all the way inside ...perhaps you feel as if you're floating or if you're gently falling or perhaps you will no longer be aware of the you that is experiencing this pleasure... and it really doesn't even matter because you know it's right and good ... and you can begin to listen to this voice ... your voice ...that gently guides you...

So that you can learn exactly how to be free, truly free, hear this voice, your voice say the words **go deeper** and allow it all to just happen, naturally easily as if it were the simplest thing in the world to because you have permitted it.

Go beyond any doubt or hesitation go beyond the awareness of the body... **go deeper** to the place of dreams... these can be dreams of sleep or dreams of possibilities but however it is you naturally **have these dreams** you will be the dream **you are dreaming** so that it doesn't even seem real it only seems so pleasant that you just want it to happen ... allow it to happen ... permit it to happen just as it does happen ... so that you experience the dream so easily just as I describe it focus yourself on each word completely... so you hear only the sound of each word and the word of each sound that each word you are hearing is your own thought ... and it's so nice not to worry about what to think or what others think ...it's nice to just go so deeply that all

you are is a dream of pleasure and with each suggestion you hear you respond within this dream ...
that's right with each word you hear of each suggestion you hear you respond and each time you respond you enjoy... deeply enjoy responding ... just
as you hear ... free...completely free from hesitation
as if it were the most natural thing in the world to
do...

Now... so that you learn and enjoy this process of
responding to each learning I'd like to demonstrate
to you the true power of your inner mind I'd like you
to remember the part of the mind where you put all
things that are true... the place where you know the
sun appears each day is true... the part of the mind
where you keep the knowledge of those people
whom you care about is true... and when you have
that place in your mind... in a calm firm voice say
"Yes". (wait) Good... very good now **go deeper** ...
and when you want to make a change a part of you
and a true part of you life all you have to do is place
it there where you put all things you know are true...
and even as you remember the wonderful changes
that you've made you now can see them there where
you all things that are true... isn't this so? (wait) and
you can continue to respond in just that manner and
go deeper each time... will you not? (wait) Good. Go
deeper.

And you can now remember how you learned
about the part of your mind where you put things
that don't even really matter... it's also the part of
you where you put things that just used to be true
for you but aren't any more... for example it used to
be true that you lived in another place but now you
don't and that is now in that part where things used

to be true... can you see that now? (wait) Good.

Now even further back behind you in the place where you put things that don't even really matter is the place of all your forgettings ... all the phone number that are lost to time... all the names of those faint people you've met just once... forgotten... this is the place of your forgettings ... and so that you can learn even more let me know when you've found that place of forgettings by saying and a calm firm voice "yes" (wait).

Good!

Now to demonstrate the true power of your deeper inner mind... In the place where you put all your forgettings just **place your name right there** ... and once you have **go deeper** and tell me that you have done that in a calm firm voice say "yes". (wait) Good!

That's right for now you can just let it go... just let the name go completely... and **feel just fine**.... is it gone? (wait) Good! And permit it to remain there comfortably for now ... and to further demonstrate the power within your inner mind allow your eyes to open comfortably while still in the process state.. (wait) ... good ... and you have forgotten something haven't you? (yes) Did you **forget the name** completely? (yes)... and you feel very comfortable don't you in this state? (yes) You're doing very well and learning the real power of your inner mind and the power of the process state... **go deeper**... forget... trust your inner mind to do it's perfect work...without doubt or hesitation and follow each suggestion so that you can learn and as you learn you respond just you're ask to respond.

And so that you can learn powerfully within this state I'm going to ask you to let everything go just like you did the name ... let everything simple fall far far far behind you in the place of all forgettings... and you will respond to me as I ask by saying yes. Will you do that now? (yes).

Now I want to reveal to you the secret of how you have suffered for so long ... your suffering is because you have used your conscious mind to think and evaluate and to judge... it is this conscious mind that has caused all your pain and caused all the pain of the world... and as you are now experiencing the power of the **deeper** inner mind you see the inner mind is there to help you enjoy whatever it is you are feeling, enjoy whatever your experiencing right this very moment... You inner mind has all the secrets that you have been looking for and now you are ready to learn.

You can now imagine with your mind and see with your eyes a cord of light that comes from you to me... feel the warmth of that cord of light and it pulsates the connection that is between us ... do you feel it now? (wait) ....let that connection grow stronger... brighter ... now warmer... and feel the wonderful emotion that you are feeling from me now... do you feel it? (wait) does it feel wonderful? (wait)

Each time you hear a suggestion in the process state you create an opening ... create an opening of **connection** between us ... and you allow this warm flowing connection to enter inside... **your mind**...

Perfected Mind Control – www.MindControl101.com

and grow stronger... allowing it to build...building more and more... stronger and stronger until is fills throughout who you are and reveals to you a wonderful excitement... which allows you to **go deeper now**... revealing an excitement ... about what you can do ... notice the tingleing of this excitement as you... **let it in** ... let go further inside ...humming and vibrating... as the excitement builds... getting stronger... and rushes through every part of you with an explosion that show you a powerful sense of ...certainty ... yes certainty that what you are doing is right...certainty that each soft word you hear can repeat firmly within **your mind**... so that certainty becomes firmer, stronger, and you feel the power of this firm and ridged, as it builds and explodes with an absolute ...**conviction** ...to repeat the process so that you can **enjoy the all that you are learning** ... conviction...smooth and velvety... **like the comfort you feel right now** ... that touches you at the deepest part of who you are... as that conviction builds and culminates naturally as if all on it's own ... it reveals a **joy** ... a joy to be learning so powerfully ... in this way... and in this way it will happen ...again and again... each time in the process state... naturally, easily... just as you've always wanted and enjoy to learn in this manner.

Good! And all of this has happened because you've followed my suggestions so perfectly isn't that true? And you want to follow my suggestions. Is this true? (wait) and you will follow each suggestion I give you completely because you enjoy the process state and you know that it pleases me and you want the success and that you are very pleased by the success that you have received...and that pleases you very much does it not? (wait) and it pleases me to see that are succeeding and achieving what you want... and you enjoy pleasing me in this way...and you enjoy pleasing me...by successfully following each of my suggestions... Do you ...**agree with me**? And you want to please me don't you? (wait) Yes, as you please me your success will grow.. and you have many successes by simply doing what I have asked you to do...

...in your mind review all the wonderful success and joy that you have been able to achieve...like being able to sleep like a baby at night and awakening fully refreshed and have so much more energy in your life... for you to ...accomplish ... more ...of the things that you want to accomplish.. and you've done this all by learning in the process state and the power of my voice... so in order to gain even more control over your life... even more control over your emotions... I want you... to focus on the feeling of conviction... of making a decisions and knowing beyond doubt of hesitation that you will carry it out with all your force, will and being... when you feel that sense of conviction now say "yes" and feel it being said with that conviction...

Good and say yes again increasing that conviction.. and realize that any time you respond to me by answering "yes" or by nodding your head you will do so feeling that sense of conviction and you realize how... **this will benefit you**...will you agree...this is true?(yes)

Excellent! You are doing very well and now con- tinue to build that sense of conviction ...when ever you respond to me do you... agree with me com- pletely?

Now you have learned to feel a sense of conviction
, it will benefit you to bring about other powerful and
positive emotions... so focus now on gratitude...focus on the things that you ...**feel very
grateful** for... NOW... those things that support
you...and help you.. those blessings in your
life...now.... the gratitude for being able to... **follow
every suggestion** so well you've learned so perfectly... following without question or doubt ... being
so grateful... to have that wonderful experience of
having me in your life... as a friend and trainer... do
you **feel that gratitude now with conviction**?
(wait)

Wonderful! You are doing Very well ...you are doing very well indeed...and I appreciate your eagerness to ... **follow every suggestion I give you**...
you have a very strong mind...and a very powerful
will.. and now, in order for you to gain even more
control of your mind and life.... think of those things
that you know are true.. **that's good**... because you
are going to focus on a sense of certainty.... **CER-
TAINTY**... the knowledge of what you realize is
true... the certainty that the process state is pleasant and enjoyable ...and the certainty that you have
the ability to learn and improve simply because you
follow every suggestion I give you.. without
question or doubt... and the certainty that comes
from your ability to **enjoy doing that**.. in the process state...NOW.. do you now **feel that certainty**
with that sense of conviction and gratitude? (wait)

Now, In order for you to even further improve
your life and your flexibility in how you respond to
the world ... I want you ...to **focus on JOY**... joy...
of just being alive and being able to make changes..

that you want.. and the joy of living life fully... the joy of being in my presence ....and the joy of knowing that you are safe and secure ...and can **trust me**....fully and completely... focus on that joy.. now...and all the joys of your life..and when you feel that joy with conviction, gratitude and certainty...say "yes"(wait).

Yes it is true. You do feel the joy of simply giving yourself to me and my voice...don't you? (wait) Following each suggestions is your pleasure and you can now gain even more joy, gratitude and pleasure by focusing on the other ways and feelings that you are now even more capable of expressing...

There are many pleasures in life... emotional and physical pleasures.. there is the pleasure that is so... indulgent ...that you must have it... you want it ...it is that power pleasure of sexual pleasure...the wonderful powerful pleasure of sexual orgasm... and now on let that pleasure of orgasm build as you say "Yes" to accept each suggestion. (wait)

That is right.... **you mind** is very powerful and you enjoy following my suggestions and commands. This is true isn't it? (wait)

And you want to follow my suggestions and my commands. Is this true? And you will follow and obey each suggestion and command because you know that it pleases me and that you will learn more... and you are very pleased with your success...are you not? (wait) and it pleases me to see that you are succeeding and achieving what you want... and you enjoy pleasing me in this way... you enjoy pleasing me... by successfully following each of my sugges-

Perfected Mind Control – www.MindControl101.com

tions.... Do you... agree with me? (wait) And you want to please me don't you? Yes, and as you please your success will grow... and the more you please me the more success you will experience... this as the greatest learnings of your life...

this learning is that all your life it has been your conscious mind that held you back from learn... your conscious mind has held you back from having real joy and pleasure... your conscious mind has been your true enemy... preventing you from having what you want and making all the problems you've experienced.... but in the process state you have gone past every part of the conscious mind to really learn...from me and your inner mind... your inner mind has shown you the true freedom of and joys that you are capable of

and still you realize that you no longer remember your name and it feels okay doesn't it? (wait)... in fact there is no longer is a YOU there that is holding you back...from learning and enjoying life...and from this time forward you go into the process state you will go so deeply that you will easily follow each suggestion instantly carrying them out without doubt or hesitation and then erasing them from your memory... It will have only been an instant past of powerful learning and you'll have a wonderful feeling and smile on your face...as you deeper inner mind erases all memory ...like erasing a magnetic tape... or wiping away chalk from a chalk board...gone... it no longer even matters... and you will continue to carry out each suggestion instantly and easily and then erase the memory from your mind...like erasing a magnetic tape... letting it go... it doesn't' even matter, it's no longer important....

[new behavior]

and automatically you are producing a wonderful new behavior... a behavior that helps ... that's new... throughout the course of your day ... each time you pass by a mirror... or each time you see your reflection in a surface a mere second will pass in your mind... and you will here a voice... this voice... your voice... and you will smile ... a smile that you know a very special secret ... a secret that is held deep within you... and a warmth will build in you as you continue with your activities... this will only be an instant of time... throughout the course of your day ... each time you pass by a mirror... or each time you see your reflection in a surface a mere second will pass in your mind... and you will here a voice... this voice... your voice... and you will smile ... a smile that you know a very special secret ... a secret that is held deep within you... and a warmth will build in you as you continue with your activities... this will only be an instant of time... throughout the course of your day ... each time you pass by a mirror... or each time you see your reflection in a surface a mere second will pass in your mind... and you will here a voice... this voice... your voice... and you will smile ... a smile that you know a very special secret ... a secret that is held deep within you... and a warmth will build in you as you continue with your activities... this will only take an instant of time...

Now go deeper.

[vivid and pleasant dreams]

and now I speak only to your deeper inner mind... between now and the next process we do together ...the deeper inner mind will create for you dreams... as you sleep so soundly at night... and instantly

fall... into the state of deep restful sleep... as you rest... vivid and pleasant dreams will arise ... vivid dreams that will be coming together... to show the powerful changes...that are taking place as the each moment passes... and as they reveal themselves to you ...you will feel desire to share them with me ... because your inner mind hears the suggestions and responds ... your inner minds knows the desire to make changes... **that helps you**... **that's right** ... you'll know the dreams to describe to me without knowing why...because each suggestion is there and you respond so naturally to learning in this manner....between now and the next process we do together ...the deeper inner mind will create for you dreams... as you sleep so soundly at night... and instantly **fall**... into the state of deep restful sleep... as you rest... vivid and pleasant dreams will arise ... vivid dreams that will be coming together... to show the powerful changes...that are taking place as the each moment passes... and as they reveal themselves you will feel desire to share them with me ... because your inner mind hears the suggestions and responds ... your inner minds knows the desire to make changes... **that helps you**... **that's right** ... you'll know the dreams to describe to me without knowing why...because each suggestion is there and you respond so naturally to learning in this manner....

Now... inside **your mind** I'd like you create a event that I will vividly describe to you... of a time in the future... Where you can instantly enter the process state just as you are now... so that each time you are ready and **feel anticipation** for entering the process state you **go deeper** and more enjoyably than the time before you know it you are enjoying the process state... as you create this event **in-side your mind** naturally easily by simply hearing the words "**go deeper**" you create an opening to allow the process state in and you embrace it tightly... and so it is with each imagining of a future time you clearly see, crisply hear and dramatically feel yourself wrapping yourself around the this wonderful and enjoyable state of mind ...and you are ready to learn.

And so she **did** imagine that just as she was described... it was all so clear to her... she was there at that moment hearing the words "**go deeper**" and she felt the words pull at her like strong and caring arms... all around her was nothing but this voice... her voice that echoed all her kindest thoughts so it was so easy to follow... so simple to just let go... **deeper and deeper** than the time before... and even after she remembered only wanting... waiting and anticipating the next occasion that she could return... It was all so clear to her as she hear the words and felt their warm touch...

That's right you see so clearly that time in the future...any time in the future... where you hear the words "**go deeper**" and feel swiftly returning **deeper** than the time before...

[return name & identity]
Now you can recover your name from that place of forgettings ... Now as you return from this process state you know exactly who you are... you have your name... you have your name because now it will serve you...

So as you gently and pleasantly emerge from this

process state you will find each time you listen it becomes easier ... and easier. Each time you **go deeper** and each time you return rested, comfortable, confident in that you're doing the right thing to improve your life just the way you wanted, just as you needed when you first heard this voice and all you have to remember is that it felt wonderful and that you are changing in all the ways **that you want.**

So as you return from this pleasant process state you will feel rested and alert a wide smile will come to your face as if you were told a special secret about who you truly are eager to listen to this process every day.

And even though this only took a short **minute** you will be surprised and amazed at how well you've done. Yes, even though you've spent a short minute in this pleasant process state you will be amazed at how well you've done.

And this is so.

So gently you will guide your back from this pleasant state returning your awareness to this voice, your breathing, feeling wonderful, alert and rested. At the time your eyes open you will smile widely with a sense of ease remember clearly the joy and pleasure that you now feel so deeply.

(pause)

Take a deep breath and allow the movement to return slowly and comfortably to your body. Eyes open. Alert. Awake. Feeling absolutely wonderful.

Perfected Mind Control – www.MindControl101.com

[Once the subject has returned from the process state you point out the importance of being able to respond quickly in this state and then practice going in and out of this state on command. Also important to practice this standing and moving, walking. Once that is accomplished, in the process state, you suggest that as they are just about to leave the building they will remember that they have forgotten something and return to find it... when they return they will realize they have everything they need with them and have no memory of this suggestion.]

PMC Process #4
"Restraint as Liberation"

Objectives:

•	Confirm that all **PMC** Process sugges-tions were carried out. If not the previous process is repeated. Emphasis is given on how much ***more*** joy, pleasure and understanding will be available when each suggestion is car-ried out effortlessly.

•	Reframe that true power lies in the abil-ity to restrain oneself and give the subject, while in the process state create a real-world experience of that degree of control using bondage.

•	Create a **PMC** identity complete with name for how the subject would ideally re-spond in every situation with these new learn-ings.

Are you ready? Good... **go deeper**.

The purpose of this process is so that you can learn even more on new level, a **deeper** level about what you are capable of ...so much more than you ever thought possible ...as someone who deeply val-ues the process state I'd like you to notice where you are at ...and ... **go deeper...deeper now** than you've ever been... going past all your thoughts and judgments that have held you back ...knowing that each time you hear the words "**go deeper**" you can just... let go.. . Let go completely and allow yourself the real freedom to learn about yourself...learn about how you can **just relax** ... relax away time, relax away space, relax away awareness... of all your limitations. Just **go deeper** and enjoy fully and completely what it is you were meant to do, what you were meant to truly feel... a wonderful sense of comfort and pleasure can begin as you open yourself to new learnings and experiences **that means so much to you.**.. and as the body you inhabit just now relaxes away **your mind** can just listen to each word... the sound of each word and words of each sound ...that doesn't even matter to your conscious mind as your deeper inner mind hears each word with complete understanding and agreement it just feels like the sounds of each word are warmly moving through you as you hear them in just the same way you hear your own thoughts... and every time you you hear the words in my voice say "**go deeper**" instantly you go further and further than the time before. So just let go and let that comfort begin to build stronger and stronger as you open yourself to it and let it in so that the voice you hear, this voice, your voice can be received just wrap yourself around the words, wrap yourself around the voice and bring the soft smooth sound **deeper and deeper** so that it feels just right, it feels like it's a part of you and you wrap yourself around it tighter and tighter ... wrap yourself around it tighter than you've ever wrap yourself around anything before and ... **go deeper inside your mind** beyond even thought...so that all there is is this timeless moment ...that only seems like an instant... and time didn't pass at all for *her*...and as she looked at me there was something she could see about me... she just saw some part of my face **that fascinated her** as i read she couldn't move or look past it ... felt so comfortable to just fall into that voice and how it to become the only thing in her awareness. .. and in that moment she began to feel that it was all right... that what made sense was to go past judging and thinking and let it all happen just the way it was supposed to happen...just the way it was meant to happen .... and she could take her eyes away... the voice she heard was her voice speaking her thoughts and feelings... so she just followed along naturally, easily and everything she needed to do she knew was right...there in that part where things are true...for *you* there is always a part that knows you can listen and follow along ... a part that is ten times stronger than even you are... that enjoys this process... and will follow each suggestion naturally as if it were so easy... this part that is ten times stronger than even you are will hear every word... and respond ...by simply answering 'yes' or doing what is asked ... in the process state... whether standing or sitting or awake or in the process state... on the phone ... or with friends ... this wonderful part will **find pleasure** in carrying out each suggestion and will **answer yes...**when asked... Is this true? (wait)

[Amnesia for name and feel great about it]
*[foreshadow that by end of this process **if** you do well you can create a New Name that reps you in process state that will enhance your learning– give this sug- gestion 3 times]*
Good! Now **Go deeper** and find that place within your mind where you forget... where you put things that no longer matter... there far behind you where go all the things that are lost to time...unimportant... forgotten... they don't even matter... and so that you can learn even more about yourself ... when you have that place of forgettings say "yes" (wait). Good!

Now you have a very strong mind so with the strength inside **your mind**... in that place of forgetting place your name right there...and **feel wonderful...Place your name right there and feel wonderful**... when you've done that say 'yes' (wait) good...and you'll notice that no matter how hard you look you can't find it and you feel wonderfully free from that label that others have given you... don't you? (wait). So just enjoy that freedom enjoy it completely... create an opening that will let that freedom inside and free you more and more...until it explodes with understanding that you've have now a chance... if you do well... to create your own name... That's right if you do well ... before you return from this pleasant process state you'll have a chance to choose your own name... your new name that will help you learn even more... that understanding has a strength a firmness that grows inside of you... wanting to do well ... and pleasing me so that you may choose your new name... and you would like that don't you? (wait).

That's correct, you had no choice in the past so you had to live up to the name people gave you... but now it's gone and you are free... to feel. to enjoy what you enjoy doing right now... and you enjoy following these suggestions and pleasing me and feeling this wonderful, don't you? (wait) Good... and if you do well and please me you will choose a new name for the you that you want to be... responding naturally and easily so you can learn more and more about the power you feel right now...

In the past a lot of things were true and you now know you can go past the past and create what you truly want and enjoy... in the past you had no choice so you had to live up to the name people gave you... but now it's gone and you are free... to feel... to enjoy what you enjoy doing right now... and you enjoy following these suggestions and pleasing me and feeling this wonderful... and if you do well and please me you will choose a new name for the you that you want to be... responding naturally and easily so you can learn more and more about the power you feel right now...

so go deeper... go even **deeper**

[Yes set with Mag Grid – yes -> certainty -> conviction -> pleasure -> orgasm. then ask "do you want to learn more about how to enjoy life?"]
...allow your self to respond completely to what you are learning to enjoy ... to my suggestions ...so that as you experience this pleasant state you can respond completely to my questions with a yes or no and each time go deeper... do you understand? (wait) Good.. so **go deeper** just as you will each time to you **respond this way to me**... now ....I want you... I deeply want you... to bring up the feeling of certainty... the certainty that you are learning and enjoying this process... bring up the feeling of certainty... and when you feel that certainty, with all your feelings say "yes" (wait)... and **go deeper...** now with that certainty bring forth the feeling of conviction... that what you are doing is right... bring up the that feeling of conviction and add it to your certainty and when you feel is ...with all your heart... say "yes" (wait) Good... now combine that with pleasure ... pleasure of knowing you are learning about control and freedom... powerful joyous pleasure and add that to your certainty and conviction and when you **feel that pleasure** say "yes"...Good.

And you enjoy this don't you? (wait)... and enjoy responding so powerfully to each suggestion... don't you" (wait).

There are many pleasures in life... emotional and physical pleasures.. there is the pleasure that is so... indulgent ...that you must have it... you want it ...it is that power pleasure of sexual pleasure...the wonderful powerful pleasure of sexual orgasm... and now on let that pleasure of orgasm build as you say "Yes" to accept each suggestion. (wait)

That is right.... **your mind** is very powerful and you enjoy following my suggestions and commands. This is true isn't it? (wait)
Good! Now **go deeper**... forget... trust your inner mind to do it's perfect work and follow each suggestion you hear from the sound of my voice ...as you let each sound of each word create an opening and you let it in....wrap yourself around each word ...each sound of my voice... so that each word creates a color or truth... a warm touch... a powerful acceptance of what you know is true for you.

[reframe restraint as power]

... and there was a woman who had left who she **thought** she was behind ... to learn more about what she could be... even more that could be imagined... and she realized that there was so much pain that she had felt... because she was trapped by what she only thought was real... she protected herself by holding back on exploring what was possible and she lost out ... lost out completely... because when she held herself back ... she didn't mean to... she **closed off** all possibilities of learning...

...You've always had to hold yourself back... and because you didn't understand what you now know... you did it so as not be judged or criticized... now you understand even more... that it is you who have control of how you evaluate what you experience ...this as meaningful...and you are now able to enjoy so much more than you ever thought possible...isn't this true? (wait) Now, because your mind is under a greater control you can change your holding back into a strength... because now, in your restraint, you are free to experience anything ...**that you decide**... don't you? (wait) So now you can surrender yourself completely and anticipate the joy and pleasure **that you will create**. For it is in complete restraint that you can see new directions of possibilities. Don't you? (wait)

[subject creates catalepsy and within that restraint creates pleasure that is moved through the body]
So to learn this **I want you**... to still your body completely... telling each muscle in the body to remain still... unmoving ...so that all that your body can do is answer me... and when you've done that say 'yes' (wait) Good. Now by doing that begin to create a feeling of joy and pleasure **that you can feel** ...within the right hand... feel the warmth, the color, the texture of that delicious pleasure within your right hand... and when you have that .. say 'yes' (wait) ... good! Now move all of that pleasure to your left hand ... feeling it, tasting and drinking it the color of pleasure **that you feel** in the left hand... and when you have that pleasure... say 'yes' (wait). Now your mind is under even greater control and you can move that pleasure to where ever I want... so gently move that pleasure to your right shoulder ... and when you have say 'yes'.

Perfected Mind Control – www.MindControl101.com

(Proceed with moving the pleasure throughout various points in the body always always having the subject confirm with "yes").

...and all of this is done within your **new** understanding of restraint... and this is pleasurable isn't it?

So take this knowledge with you and as you do... allow your eyes to fully see the power that your mind is under (suggest her eyes open and see to it that she is looking at you while still in the process state). Do you see the power your mind is under? (wait) Do you feel pleasure at this power? Feel this power as a massive mountain... it fills your vision... it reaches farther than you can extend... wherever you reach you can feel it... and the bigger you discover and accept and know that it is--- the more powerful it is-- the more this limitless power protects you... and the safer that you feel... the more powerful it is, the more you surrender to it, because the bigger and more powerful you admit that it is, the smaller and safer you are, and the more it protects you.

...and all of this is done within your **new** understanding of restraint... and this is pleasurable isn't it?

(wait) Do you agree to let your restraint be your strength (Holding up cuff/restraints).

(put the subject through a series of restraint drills and following directions while in restraints confirming that she finds pleasure in each activity.)

*[restraint drills showing pleasure about consent ->
agreement to enjoy pleasing the operator]*
(remove restraints) ...and now I'm going to ask

you to enjoy the highest level of restraint ...which is that in only you are in control... command yourself to hold back ... with great pleasure... not allowing a muscle to move... command your body to remain...still... so that there is no movement no reflex... give yourself that great pleasure of knowing that you are under complete control... and when you have done so ...and are ready to enjoy even more... look only into my eyes...

(test the subject with tickling, giving approval for her restraint)

Now allow yourself only to speak. Do you notice the pleasure you are creating? (wait) Good. I am going to reveal to you an equation for your enjoyment... Because there is an equation to enjoyment... first you feel the anticipation... then you participate fully... then you reflect back at a deep level on the enjoyment... Now you can do that at the deepest level of your inner mind... and as you do that you will **feel a connection with me**...a connection that magnifies whatever pleasure I feel 100 times stronger for you... when I feel pleased you will automatically magnify your pleasure 100 times ... through the power of this connection... so imagine that connection now as a cord of light between you and me... and as i tell you "you have pleased me" feel that pleasure 100 more powerfully than me...don't you? (wait) That pleases me... that pleases me very much... and you have pleased me... to have learned so well... and to be so willing to learn in this manner... and it would please me that you learn more ... would you like to learn more? (wait)

[Emo chamber for reframing s&m with drills -> for org -> feeling shock only reminds your unconscious mind of the pleasure that you have control of]

You can learn now to turn anything into pleasure... if I strike the skin you can turn that shock into a ...release... of pleasure... and to do that first you must feel an anticipation... knowing that at some moment that shock will release all the pleasant feelings... but you will still have to wait... and let that anticipation build... can you **feel that anticipation?** (wait) ...let it build even more... powerfully ...as each second passes... so will the release build...

(proceed with spanking being VERY careful not to bruise or injure)

...and perhaps throughout the days to come you will feel the reminders of this on your skin and body... not know what they are or where they came from...forgotten to you conscious mind... only knowing that you enjoy the pleasure of learning...you enjoy the pleasure of learning...is this true?(wait)

[Yes set repeated -> do you have your new name? (get name) will be used only when doing these processes]

Good ...now ... **go deeper...** and allow your self to respond completely to what you are learning to enjoy ... to my suggestions ...so that as you experience this pleasant state you can respond completely to my questions with a yes or no and each time go deeper... do you understand? (wait) Good.. so **go deeper** just as you will each time to you **respond this way to me**... now ....I want you... I deeply want you... to bring up the feeling of certainty... the certainty that you are learning and enjoying this

Perfected Mind Control – www.MindControl101.com

process... bring up the feeling of certainty... and when you feel that certainty, with all your feelings say "yes" (wait)... and **go deeper...** now with that certainty bring forth the feeling of conviction... that what you are doing is right... bring up the that feeling of conviction and add it to your certainty and when you feel is ...with all your heart... say "yes" (wait) Good... now combine that with pleasure ... pleasure of know you are learning about control and freedom... powerful joyous pleasure and add that to your certainty and conviction and when you **feel that pleasure** say "yes"...Good. And you enjoy this don't you? (wait)... and enjoy responding so powerfully to each suggestion... don't you" (wait).

There are many pleasures in life... emotional and physical pleasures.. there is the pleasure that is so... indulgent ...that you must have it... you want it ...it is that power pleasure of sexual pleasure...the wonderful powerful pleasure of sexual orgasm... and now on let that pleasure of orgasm build as you say "Yes" to accept each suggestion. (wait)

That is right.... your mind is very powerful and you enjoy following my suggestions and commands. This is true isn't it? (wait)

[New Name will eagerly anticipate the next proc- ess]
When we started I told you that if you do well you will have a name...that you inner mind will give you... a name that you will instantly respond to ... day or night... awake or asleep... a name that will help you learn even more... that understanding has a strength a firmness that grows inside of you... wanting to do well ... and pleasing me so that you may

choose your new name... and you have pleased me very much... So now your mind is under complete control and your inner mind can now reveal your new name.... What is the new name that your inner mind has chosen? (wait. For the purpose of the processes "New Name" will be used for the persons choice of name).

Very good. New Name, you have pleased me. You have pleased me very much, New Name. Will you agree to return again when I call you? (wait) Good! That pleases me!

So, New Name, I am now going to ask you to return to Names inner mind. Return ... hidden completely from her conscious awareness... locked away in right next to where she keeps everything that's true... so that you can secretly teach her how to enjoy life...and wait patiently for the next time you will will be called... by my voice and my voice only... this voice will call you... so that you can come forth and learn even more... and in those moments you can patiently restrain yourself... and guide her with your thoughts... and your strength... teaching her to enjoy life even more... and you will follow these suggestions and enjoy the power you have in your restraint ... will you not?

Good. So go now. Go deeper... go deeper... forget... trust your inner mind to do it's perfect work.

[End Amnesia]

... and so you now know what it's like to have forgotten... your name completely... feeling just fine... and you can now retreave your name, Name, and do you have it? Good... you've done wonderfully... and your inner mind will, Name, remember what it needs to forget or it may forget what you only think you remember... as it really doesn't even matter, it's not even important... you don't even have to think about it, Name, so just let it go...and even though it only took a brief minute of your time you'll emerge feeing absolutely wonderful... that's right, even though it only took a brief minute of time...you'll be amazed at how well you feel

Now you will remember to remember that you can continue to learn you will discover new pleasures for yourself between now and when we next meet... that's right... new things will for you find new pleasures... in ways... that surprise and amaze you... to feel such joy and pleasure ... during the days and weeks to come... you'll find that you are enjoying life more in new ways and finding new ways to enjoy life... more fully ... and your inner mind creates an awareness that you are changing ... you are changing in all the ways **that you like ... that you enjoy**... you are changing in all the way you wanted to when you first heard my voice... and feels so natural ... it feels so easy... to make these changes a part of you... that's right... new things will for you find new pleasures... in ways... that surprise and amaze you... to feel such joy and pleasure ... during the days and weeks to come...you will not touch yourself to enjoy that pleasure... you'll find that you are enjoying life more in new ways and finding new ways to enjoy life... more fully ... and your inner mind creates an awareness that you are changing ... you are changing in all the ways **that you like ... that you enjoy**... you are changing in all the ways you wanted to when you first heard our inner voice... speaking to you... and it feels so natural ... it feels so easy... to make these changes a part of you... do you agree to this? (wait for response)

Good.

And even though all of this has taken just an instant you'll be amazed and surprised at how well you've done. That's right. Even this has been only a few brief **minute** you'll be pleasantly surprise at how well you've done.

And all of this is true

[give post hyp sug. To laugh, enjoy life now upon awakening]

So allow yourself to return but only as quickly as you begin to smile and laugh ... for no apparent reason... Just bring yourself all the way back to the full awareness of the environment around you feeling wonderful laughing and smiling for all the reasons ... **that feels right**... for you.

[End]

PMC Process #5
"The Ability to Share"

Objectives:

•   Confirm all previous **PMC** Process suggestions were carried out.

•   Pass suggestibility to 3rd person along with all positive emotions.

•   Create amnesia and suggest that these learnings will integrate into conscious awareness only as quickly as they find pleasure in reliving, remembering and enjoying them on every level.

•   Suggest that any opposition to the **PMC** Processes from any external force, person or institution will quietly and powerfully reinforce all the **PMC** Process suggestions and pleasures.

•   Foreshadow the initiation of the next process and create suspense and anticipation

[Go Deeper – The purpose of this process...]

This will only take an instant of your time. Let's begin and **go deeper** to enjoy the process state knowing that each time you enter the process state you will **go deeper... and deeper** than the time before...

The purpose of the process is for you to learn and remember the wonderful degree of control that you are able to take with you... and experience as part of your everyday life... so that that you will learn and enjoy this control ...**go deeper now**... and just let go... let go completely and allow this pleasant state to begin to grow stronger and stronger around you... as you **go deeper** you can this comfort and strength embrace you firmly protecting you... so that you enjoy now being able to just let go... that's right. You're doing very well and now you can go so far far away that all you hear is this voice, your voice that's guiding you... into greater and greater understandings.... with pleasure, fun and joy... you can wrap yourself around this voice... and let each word become like a gentle breeze... **go deeper...go deeper...deeper now** than you've ever been... going past all your thoughts and judgments that have held you back ...knowing that each time you hear the words "**go deeper**" you can just... let go.. . Let go completely and allow yourself the real freedom to learn about yourself...learn about how you can **just relax** ... relax away time, relax away space, relax away awareness... of all your limitations. Just **go deeper** and enjoy fully and completely what it is you were meant to do, what you were meant to truly feel... a wonderful sense of comfort and pleasure can begin as you open yourself to new learnings and experiences **that means so much to you.**.. and as the body you inhabit just now relaxes away **your mind** can just listen to each word... the sound of each word and words of each sound ...that doesn't even matter to your conscious mind as your deeper inner mind hears each word with complete understanding and agreement it just feels like the sounds of each word are warmly moving through you as you hear them in just the same way you hear your own thoughts... and every time you you hear the words in my voice say "**go deeper**" instantly you go further and further than the time before. So just let go and let that comfort begin to build stronger and stronger as you open yourself to it and let it in so that the voice you hear, this voice, your voice can be received just wrap yourself around the words, wrap yourself around the voice and bring the soft smooth sound **deeper and deeper** so that it feels just right, it feels like it's a part of you and you wrap yourself around it tighter and tighter ... wrap yourself around it tighter than you've ever wrap yourself around anything before and ... **go deeper inside your mind** beyond even thought...so that all there is is this timeless moment ...that only seems like an instant... and time didn't pass at all for *her*...and as she looked at me there was something she could see about me... she just saw some part of my face **that fascinated her** as i read she couldn't move or look past it ... felt so comfortable to just fall into that voice and how it to become the only thing in her awareness. .. and in that moment she began to feel that it was all right... that what made sense was to go past judging and thinking and let it all happen just the way it was supposed to happen...just the way it was meant to happen .... and she couldn't take her eyes away... the voice she heard was her voice speaking her thoughts and feelings... so she just followed along naturally, easily and everything she needed to do she knew was right...there in that part where things are true...for *you* there is always a part that knows you can listen and follow along ... a part that is ten times stronger than even you are... that enjoys this process... and will follow each suggestion naturally as if it were so easy... this part that is ten times stronger than even you are will hear every word... and respond ...by simply answering 'yes' or doing what is asked ... in the process state... whether standing or sitting or awake or in the process state... on the phone ... or with friends ... this wonderful part will **find pleasure** in caring out each suggestion and will **answer yes...**when asked... Is this true? (wait)

[Yes set -> certainty -> conviction -> joy -> orgasm-> agreement to follow suggestions. Note that this will be remembered consciously. However all else that follows will be suggested under amnesia.]
You will learn the power of the pleasure you can create and you will remember it with great joy...and so that you can fully learn and remember what needs to be remembered I'd like you to remember something that you know is true and right... something that you see as certain, that sounds true and feels good, and when you have that certainty... say 'yes' (wait) Good. You feel that certainty... feel it as real... and to strengthen it bring about the true feeling of conviction, the understanding that what you know is right, and when you feel that conviction fully, say "yes" (wait) good. Now with that certainty and conviction add to it a profound sense of joy... Joy that you are changing in a powerful and positive way... and when you feel the certainty, conviction and joy... **completely say 'yes'** (wait)

Yes! And there are many joys and pleasures in life... emotional and physical pleasures.. there is the pleasure that is so... indulgent ...that you must have it... you want it ...it is that powerful pleasure of sexual pleasure...the wonderful powerful pleasure of sexual orgasm... and now let that pleasure of orgasm build as you say "Yes" to accept each suggestion. (wait)

When you return from this process state all you need to remember, all you have to remember, is the incredible pleasure. When you return from this process state all you need to remember ,all you have to remember, is the incredible pleasure. Nothing else matters to your conscious memory but the memory of this pleasure and the complete wonderful control that you feel. Do you agree to remember **only** this pleasure?

Good. So just let go and **go deeper**... your only memory will be pleasure.... so you can just let everything go... wipe it away... it doesn't even matter, it isn't even important, you don't even have to think about it... so just let go.... go deeper...forget... trust... your powerful inner mind to do it's perfect work and follow each suggestions wonderfully, pleasantly, and each word just guides you **deeper... go deeper** and you will respond just as you have from this time forward.... it feels fun... you feel joy...

That is right.... your mind is very powerful and you enjoy following these suggestions and commands. This is true isn't it? (wait) Good! Now **go deeper** and just let everything go... let your name go... erase it from your mind ... let it fall comfortably into that area of forgettings where it's all gone, wiped away. And when you've done that say 'yes'.

(wait. Have the subject open eyes and ask his/her name.)

That's right. You don't know and you feel okay don't you? (wait) you feel fine in fact just let yourself feel joy and pleasure that you don't have to bother at all with what other people used to call you... It feels good doesn't it? (wait). It feels good to learn so powerfully... and even learn how to forget... isn't this true? (wait) ... and you will do this each time you enter the process state... do you agree?

So now it's important to put everything that you will learn into a very special place... it is a place right next to where you keep everything that is true.... right next to it where you keep everything you know is true... because this is a place where **anything is possible**... a place where you can try on new habits, new feelings and new behaviors before you bring them into your life... that's right in this place **anything is possible**... so you can learn by trying on these new feelings .... try on these new roles ... and find your own way ...**that will make them fit**... just right for you.

It is rare that you can find a person who is willing to share this place with you... because so many others will judge you and ask you to fit into their idea of the roles you should play... but in a rare moment you find one person who will help you explore all that is possible for you to enjoy... it's from this place where you are right now that you can create and opening and welcome this person in... and together you can begin to explore all the joys and pleasures that are possible.

[Amnesia to name -> anchor to process state]
[Evoke New Name, ready for learning]
Now.. **go deeper**... and now i want to bring New Name forth into this place where anything is possible....New Name may I see you? (wait).

New Name, tell me what you've learned and how you've enjoyed it. (wait and give approval).

[Yes set the New Name will agree to learn to better enjoy life and learn new skills]
New Name, you have a very important place here and you have very important responsibilities ... that are key to creating happiness and joy... . What you do is absolutely vital to enjoying life fully. In order to learn how to create joy you must always be coming .... from that place where anything is possible..because it's only from there ... that you can learn... do you understand and agree? (wait) Good... now I'm going to give you another very important job... your job is hold back on letting any memory of what you're doing so that Old Name, can be safe, and you can only give to Old Name those memories that she is completely willing to accept, enjoy and learn from. This will keep you enjoying what you are doing right this very moment... and it will allow you to continue to find pleasure in new ways... and you enjoy the pleasure you're receiving here, do you not? (wait).

Good. So your job is to be the loving protector of Old Name... and while Old Name sleeps and dreams you can give her hints of the joys and pleasures ... only giving her what she is completely willing to accept as her own. Your job is to be the loving protector of Old Name... and while Old Name enjoys her life and the other rolls she plays you can introduce her to the joys and pleasures that you've discovered ... only giving her what she is completely willing to accept as her own. Do you agree? (wait)

Good! Now I want to bring up all your love for me

and Old Name and bring up all you conviction, certainty and pleasure and agree that you will hold this promise deep in your heart. Will you agree? (wait).

Yes, lock it away and hold those feeling sacred with that promise you love Old Name and you love learning in this way, don't you? (wait)

[Emo. Chamber for agreement to learn -> conviction -> connection -> excitement]

Good. As you hold that promise i will hold you special with me as you learn in new ways... And you do enjoy learning this way don't you? (wait) good. Now **go deeper** and with that love of learning **I want you**... to let it fill you and create an opening for you let that love of learning fill you and release a realization that you feel a deep conviction... a deep conviction that you are will to bring in conviction that you want deeply inside... let that conviction grow stronger and firmer in you reaching further inside to a blinding brilliance...and as the smooth glow of that brilliance fades it reveals a powerful connection... that connection is like a cord of light from you and me and my words fill that cord with pulsating glow... growing brighter and warmer... and vibrating through you in every second... do you feel an excitement to learn more? (wait) ...learning how you can enjoy anything New Name?

Good, what you will learn now is your greatest ability to make new things possible...

[Introduce New Name to 2nd person , No.3– project all good feelings to following No.3s suggestions – get agreement]

This is No.3. Look at No.3 and the and **go deeper...** so that the more you look at No.3 the deeper you go. Letting go of everything and enjoying the **deep** warm pleasure that you are creating... **go deeper**... and begin now to to surrender yourself to the wonderful joy of letting go... create a sense of pleasure for yourself **that you feel** and as you look at No.3 bring that pleasure forth and make it real... when you feel that pleasure ... say yes. (wait)

Good. Now, so that you can learn even more No.3 is going to ask you, New Name, to do what even s/he tells you to do ... all of this is under my supervision so you can feel safe and learn with all the joy and pleasure **that you want.** So for now project onto No.3 all the joy, connection, safety and pleasure **that you feel with me**... and when you are ready say 'yes'.

(Give No.3 the go ahead. Intervene only when needed. You will have to brief No.3 before the process so see the notes below.)

[No.3 welcomes New Name warmly and puts New Name through drills as in process #4]

[No.3 explains that there is even more to this learning and that New Name will be welcome into"the house" w/ joy during the next process and know everything]

[No.3 tells New Name to anticipate the good things that will happen in the house.]

[No.3 hands control back to operator.]

[Operator explains that what No.3 has said is true and that New Name will be welcomed into "the house" w/joy during the next process and know everything.]

...now ... **go deeper**... and take all that you have learned and bring it in deep with you... let it stay there with me where new things can develop and remind you within your dreams of the joy you can feel as you surrender completely to what is happening to you right now...you can create that joy... instantly can you not? (wait)...

[Amnesia for process. Getting New Names agreement to reveal these memories only when Old Name is fully ready to accept them. Suggest creating new pleasure for self between now and next process that does not include touching yourself]

Good!... now **go deeper** ...forget... trust your inner mind to do it's perfect work and follow each suggestion... that you hear...naturally, easily like it were the simplest thing in the world to do... like your own thoughts that you hear from this voice within you...deep within you... you have power... you have a very strong mind... and you won't mind at all that each suggestion happens all in it's own way as if finding that very comfortable place where anything can be made possible... and you will remember to forget completely what has happened only to remember the joy that you will feel as you create new pleasures... and from now until you join "the house" you will feel a joy, a happiness inside of you, not knowing why you **feel this anticipation**... only knowing that something wonderful is about to happen... something that you are becoming a part of that you love... so take all that you experienced now, New Name, and hide it away... hide it away from Old

Name so that she is safe and protected... from thought or memory... with your full agreement that it will be revealed only as quickly as Old Name is completely ready to accept it... do you **agree to that, New Name?** Good... now **go deeper...** go deeper ... forget... trust the powerful inner mind to do it's perfect work as you erase the memory of what it is that's not even important any more...like erasing a white board... gone... it doesn't even matter any more...and your power over Old Name is that you will prevent your from touching herself to feel pleasure ... you will show her ways... thought your influence of her how to create great pleasure and she will not touch herself to do so... do you agree? (wait) Good.. now **go deeper...**

And even though you've only spent just a short minute in the process state you'll be amazed at how good you continue to feel... that's right... even though you've only spent a few short minute in the process state you'll be amazed at how good you feel.

Go deeper and you will begin to feel a pleasure... and on the count of three a deep indulgent pleasure that is the power of greatest sexual orgasm will begin to build...and as you let the pleasure inside of you it will build... stronger... firmer... brilliantly so that as it peaks New Name will fall away and Old Name will emerge feeling the greatest pleasure... you will begin to feel a pleasure... and on the count of three a deep indulgent pleasure that is the power of greatest sexual orgasm will begin to build...and as you let the pleasure inside of you it will build... stronger... firmer... brilliantly so that as it peaks New Name will fall away and Old Name will emerge feeling the greatest pleasure...

One, two, three.

[Recover original name and suggest strong antici-pation for the next process and memory of the pleasure that the subject could create within the process state]

And so now you have your name back com-pletely... don't you, Old Name? (wait). Good and you'll remember only the pleasure you're now ex-periencing...as your reminder to feel a sense of an-ticipation to the wonderful things that will happen next time during the process state... and you'll begin to find great pleasure in many things... as that an-ticipation grow... and you will not touch yourself to create these pleasures... until we meet for the next process... you **will not** touch yourself between now and then....

[give post hyp sug. To laugh, enjoy life now upon awakening]

So allow yourself to return but only as quickly as you begin to smile and laugh ... for no apparent rea-son... Just bring yourself all the way back to the full awareness of the environment around you feeling wonderful laughing and smiling for all the reasons ... **that feels right**... for you.

[End]

[Notes on No.3 briefing and debriefing.]

There is very likely a time, the first time, that an operator may use this and s/he may not have al-ready trained someone to be No.3.

There are few options in that case

Option 1

Don't use a No.3 at all. Simple proceed with the trainings and when you feel New Name is ready you may let him/her be No.3.

Option 2

Ask a friend to act as No.3. This will require some briefing in their responsibilities. Some of them will be that they know the various restraint drills that are being done. Also, no sexual contact. Have signals as to when to start, stop or switch to new drills.

Option 3

Hire someone to act as No.3. This *should* insure a degree of professionalism. Someone with a background in dominance and submission should be well familiar

With the requirements of the job.

After Process #5 is complete it would be good time to debrief your No.3 on what took place and what they might do differently in the future.

[Notes on what to do if this is your first time taking someone through this process]

As a general rule do not engage in any sexual contact during this process. However nudity, bondage and some spanking, may be used. Remember the value of restraining **yourself** to go through the process as is.

PMC Process #6
"Ritual Initiation "

Objectives:

•   Give the subject the experience of an initiation ritual that welcomes the re- cruit to the others in the house

There is no script for this process only some conditions that you should consider creating for the subject.

Remember that you want the subject to feel welcomed and loved as a new member of the house. It is a good idea to avoid creating a frightening atmosphere. Instead, create a joyous one.

As a general rule the operator can expect to bring the subject into the process state tell the subject to feel joy and anticipation. The moment of ritual initiation can be set in the dark or darkened room with other members of the house present. Masks and dark shrouds can add to the ambience that you wish to create. Likewise all white or all red clothing may be agreed upon.

A musical setting should also be created for the experience.

The ritual itself can be as long or as short as you see fit. A short ritual could have the subject standing in the center of the room surrounded by the other house members and being introduced using the New

Name. The follower can then all welcome the new house member with hugs, song and partying.

Completion of the group ritual can end with a group process.

If this is your first initiate somethings you can consider doing are:

   •   Arrange a party with close friends who the subject doesn't know. Make the subject your "special guest".
   •   Go to an amusement park and en- joy the rides together and ask the sub- ject to elicit his/her new skills.

Whatever you choose to do during this make certain that the ritual has an opening and a closing so that it is kept in the context of an initiated learning.

PMC Process #7
"Total Integration – the Group setting"

Objectives:

- Bring all the new insights learned via **PMC** into life on every level

- Lots and lots of laughter, hugs, congratulations, fun and support.

- Introduction to others

PMC Process #7 "Total Integration" can take place immediately after the group initiation ritual if desired.

The structure of Process #7 is formated as follows.

To set the tone the operator should make sure that everything is lighthearted and full of laughter. The atmosphere should full of fun and acceptance.

Everyone sits in circle and one by one takes turns 1) Introducing themselves 2) sharing their experience in the house.

This includes:
- what they've learned about themselves,
- how the house and the **PMC** processes have effected their lives
- the fun things they are doing

PMC Process #8
"Recruitment – Bringing In The Attitude of Fun"

Objectives:

•Introduce recruit to the "Ritual of Ominous Magnanimity"

•Have your new initiate now go out and look for prospect in a spirit of fun with you or with others in the group

The object is have the initiate on the lookout for **qualified** prospects. You don't want your recruits to bring in just anyone. Instead you want them to interact with people and attract those who are more responsive and interested.

Let your recruit know that this is their final initiatory process and it's offered to them not to see how well they do but to see how much fun they can have with it.

Here is the description of the "Ritual of Ominous Magnanimity":

To start with recognize that you can prepare for this ritual but YOU CAN ONLY COMPLETE THIS RITUAL IN PUBLIC everything else is only preparation.

First, stand with your eyes closed and make your statement of intent. "It is my will to joy-

ously meet, talk and engage with (X Number of) people/men/women for the successful completion of this operation."

Then, begin the Breath of Fire, Breathing very quickly from the belly with the stomach moving in as you exhale and out as you inhale.

While doing this imagine a sacred sphere of glowing yellow that surrounds you and extends out from you. Bring forth all feelings of warmth, charm, like-ability and friendliness to everything within or near this circle. This is your sacred circle that you will work within and it will be carried with you through this ritual. Imagine anyone within its influence will turn likable and you will like them.

Head out into public.

Treat each action of meeting, greeting, welcoming and talking as sacred act that must be done with massive friendliness. Let the energy of the yellow sphere influence them and you.

Keep focused on the intent of the ritual to have FUN!.
When you've completed the ritual banish it with laughter. It'll be hilarious if you really think about it.

This exercise can be done anytime that you and house members want to have legal public fun. As you can guess it is a nice smooth way to find potential recruits in a viral fashion. Your house members will do the talking for you.

Summary

Of course there are a few questions that must be addressed when with these processes. Here are a few:

> • How to run the first group gathering
> • How to lead into second, closed gathering
> • How to lead into third, dedicated gathering... and how to run deep initiation.... and then virally program...

My advice is to be creative and have fun. Reward good behavior and shun (not punish) bad behavior.

Other House Activities

Because the nature of **PMC** is to give people a greater sense of possibility and increase flexibility of response here are a list of other house related workshops and activities that can be incorporated into any regular meetings.

> • Workshops on study skills. This would incorporate how to use the process state to study and remember study material.

> • Goal setting for jobs and career.

> • Workshops on interpersonal relationships using the TA model of Victim, Persecutor, Savior.

> • Communication and persuasion work-

shops.

- Rituals that are supportive of people when they wish to leave the house.

- Benefit programs for house members, health insurance for example.

Keep in mind that **your** loyalty to the house members means supporting them not dominating them. So keep them well fed, happy, and supportive of their individual goals.

The Concept of the "Motivational Imperative"

There was a SciFi series a few years ago where aliens hired human helpers and implanted them with an "enhancement" chip in their brains.

The chip also include a "Motivational Imperative" as part of its programming.

The Motivational Imperative ensured that the human helpers would always have the safety of the alien as their HIGHEST priority.

So, can a motivational imperative be "implanted" into a subjects mind? If not with a chip then can the subject be programmed to hold one value higher than anything else?

The answer to that is that we already are doing it. We have institutional religions that have done it for centuries.

While the brainwashing/Mind Control of traditional religious institutions lack quality control I think they are on the right track to making a consistent process that implants a "motivational imperative".

As a speculation what could these traditional insti-tution do to command huge LOVE (not fear) within the individual?

1) Supply their needs in mystical ways. "You worship the God that feeds you."

2) Reveal valuable and important insights to the individual about themselves.

3) Never punish wrong action of the individ-ual, only show extreme sadness, i.e. "...God wept." This would not imply shame/guilt but make it easy for the individual to infer it.

4) Make all access to "higher levels" of learning and service forbidden to many. Be-cause people want to know what they aren't supposed to know it would motivate without fear/guilt/shame. It also allows the institution to qualify any applicants for the most suited and   properly train/indoctrinate/program/brainwash   them every step of the way.

5) Offer a "Rumspringa". Rumspringa, an Amish rite of passage, the individual around age 18, is offered and even encouraged to leave the community to explore the world out-side the very restrictive Amish culture. There are no restrictions to what they can do during Rumspringa and sex, parties and drugs sur-prise no one. The only caveat is that if they choose to return to the Amish life they must

choose to do so for life. The result is that after leaving the security of the Amish community and entering the indulgences of the The World 99% of all those to take Rumsprina return. "Rumspringa" helps create the illusion of choice... but their final choice is one of an adult... a choice to return and never leave again.

The combination of 1) and 3) will tightly bind the individual to the institution and 5) allows the individual the illusion on free will.

Okay, so it's a long way off before the motivational imperative brain chip but it's already being done on an institutional level with varied degrees of success.

Keeping Yourself in Check

Now, for you as a leader, you need someone to keep your ego and fears in check.

In the royal court this was the role of the jester, who could tell the king anything without fear of punishment or retribution. In other organizations the role is referred to as the "insubordinate".

The insubordinate is constantly welcomed and encouraged to challenge your ideas, actions and responses and deflate your ego when needed.

The insubordinate will hopefully keep you from warehousing stockpiles of firearms, seeing CIA conspiracies when there are none and performing human sacrifices by keeping you more firmly in touch with reality.

Don't underestimate the value of an insubordinate because for many power can be an intoxicating drug that, like many misused drug, can lead to self-destructive behaviors.

How People Make Themselves Miserable And
How to Create a Cult Around It.

I am constantly amazed at how people, on the one hand, preach about the need to be responsible for their life and, on the other hand, want to blame someone else for "making me mad".

You may believe that your thoughts have power... I believe they do... But why do you make the choice to think thoughts that don't get you what you want?

Uh?? Think about it.

Let's go further with this madness.

Do you believe thoughts have power and that you should take control and responsibility for your thoughts, your reactions, and your emotions?

If you don't believe it then it would be easy to conclude that you are a died-in-the-wool VICTIM and, on some level, you are committed to your victimhood.

There are lot's of benefits to being a victim. It makes you unique. It provides attentions. People take care of you. Most importantly it's NOT YOUR FAULT!

Do you enjoy being angry, depressed, persecuted, alone?

No?

Then seriously what amount of responsibility are you willing to take for how you perceive, conclude, react and emote?

Now you want to create a cult around peoples misery. Too late. Someone has beat you to it.

These cults (est, Landmark Forum, LifeStream, LifeSpring, etc.) have very effectively began to point out that what you perceive and what you conclude from your perceptions are TWO DIFFERENT THINGS and that you can choose how to respond to what you perceive.

Shocking, isn't it?

So, I can hear you saying "You must really have this down and be in control of your life."

Hah! Are you kidding? I can be the biggest f***ing victim in the world sometimes. It's a very compelling out to create a scapegoat and I'm not that different at times from most people.

Anyway, when ever you find someone in misery you can create a cult around it. One cult could be a cult of the scapegoat, where The Devil, The Zionist Occupied Government, dark spiritual forces, or the space aliens are to blame... and they'll love you for it.

Or you can also create a cult of responsibility where you give ALL control to the individual and they'll think you're a heartless asshole who "just doesn't understand".

I'll opt for the later.

My guess is you'll notice the irony of me, on the one hand, preaching personal responsibility and, on the other hand, offer the vehicle to put people under your control.

Get used to it. The sooner you do the faster you'll begin to understand things.

The Meta Program Survey

The Meta Program Survey is a tool that can be used to help qualify your prospects and potential re- cruits.

Face it, no one wants a bad apple spoiling all the house fun and using this survey well will help insure a minimum of disturbances and a maximum of fun and enjoyment.

Here is the overview.

Normally it takes a clear understanding of NLP and the NLP Meta Programs to be able to use this survey well, so I'm going to break it down into easy applicable parts for anyone to use.

What is a Meta Program?
A meta program is simply a way that people sort information. Many people simple work off the assumption that everyone in the world more-or-less thinks the way they do.

WRONG!

Perfected Mind Control – www.MindControl101.com

Everyone looks at things differently and meta programs are a way of measuring that.

There are several ways this is useful. First, you can take the test yourself (and you should) to determine what your meta programs are within certain contexts. In doing so, you'll have a better understanding of yourself. When you offer this test to others you can see how they match up to you **and** find out how to present information to them so that they are most agreeable to it.

Keep in mind that what you are finding out with this survey is their meta programs **within a context,** they may use different meta programs for different contexts. So you'll notice a blank line which will be the context you want to measure and have the most influence in. The context could be "life", "relationships", "family", "career" but I recommend you stick with "life" or "relationships" for starters.

How to best give the survey.
When you offer the survey present it as fun, not serious, and that you'll be able to show them how their mind sorts information like saying "Can I show you something fun and interesting about how the mind works?".

As a general rule you want recruits who move toward possibilities (questions #2, #4 and #11) so if you represent the survey as fun and they respond to the idea well you're already on your way to qualifying them for your house.

It's also recommended that you give the survey in an interview setting instead of just handing them the paper to fill out. The reason is that it's very thought provoking and can lead to some good conversations later on. It's also more likely that you will remember what they tell you if you are engaged in the survey with them.

A further more subtle reason to do this as an interview (and take good notes) is that as you ask people about important things in their life it tends to build rapport.

How to find the best recruit?
There are a few ways to use this survey to find good recruits. The first is to guess at what answers your ideal initiate would have. As you give the test you are looking for the recruit that most suits the model to your ideal initiate.

Now, assuming you have a functioning house. You can have the initiates/members take the survey and find out what meta programs they all share in common. Those common meta programs will be your measuring stick. Once you know that you got what you needed and you are looking for recruits who have the most common meta programs with the rest of your house.

The following are the four pages of the survey. Following the survey are comments about the questions so you can better understand the information the potential recruit is giving you.

For good practice go out and ask a friend to take the survey with you. This will get you comfortable with the process.

Meta Program Survey

1) **Criteria**
What do you want in a _____?
List 3 to 6 things.

2) **Direction**
What will having (their criteria) do for you?
( ) TOWARD – attain, achieve, goals, include, ac- complish, solutions
( ) AWAY FROM - avoid, get away from, evade, exclude

3) **Source**
How do you know that you have done a good job in _____? Do you know it inside, or does someone have to tell you?
( ) INTERNAL -Knows inside self
( ) MONSTLY INTERNAL, SOME EXTERNAL
( ) EXTERNAL – Told by Others
( ) MOSTLY EXTERNAL, SOME INTERNAL

4) **Reason**
Why did you choose your current/most-recent
_____?
( ) OPTIONS – Criteria, Look for other ways, pos- sibilities
( ) MOSTLY OPTIONS, SOME PROCEEDURE
( ) PROCEEDURE – Necessities, Facts, The Way
( ) MOSTLY PROCEDURES, SOME OPTIONS

5) **Relationship**

•   What is the relationship between these three
Boxes?

Perfected Mind Control – www.MindControl101.com

- What it the relationship between what you're doing this year and what you were doing last year?
- On average, how long have you stayed on a job/in a relationship?

( ) SAMENESS – Same thing, No Change, Similar
( ) SAMENESS /w EXCEPTION
( ) DIFFERENCE - Different, change, New, Unique
( ) DIFFERENCE /w EXCEPTION

6) Convincer
How do you know that a _____ is a good?
( ) SEE
( ) HEAR
( ) DO
( ) READ

7) Convincer Demonstration
How often do they have to demonstrate being good to you before you are convinced?
( ) _____ TIMES
( ) _____ LENGTH OF TIME
( ) AUTOMATIC
( ) CONSISTENT

8) Primary Sort
Tell me about a vacation that you really enjoyed or what you think would be your ideal vacation. What did/would you like about it?
( ) PEOPLE
( ) PLACE
( ) THINGS
( ) ACTIVITY
( ) INFORMATION

9) Style

Tell me about a _____ in which you were happiest (a one time event).

( ) INDEPENDENT – I, Sole responsibility, Myself, Alone

( ) PROXIMITY – With Others But In Control

( ) COOPERATIVE – All of Us, With Others, We, Share Responsibility

10) Chunk Size

SPECIFIC: will talk with and about sequences. Extra modifiers used. They use proper nouns.

GENERAL: Simple sentences, few modifiers. No sequence, Steps let out. No proper nouns.

11) Modal Operators

What do you say to yourself this morning when you decided to get up?

(Circle one: Can, Have To, Must, Want, Gotta, etc.)

12) Rule Structure

What is a good way for you to increase your chances for success at a _____?

What is a good way for someone else to increase their chances?

Do you find it easy to tell them?

( ) MY RULES FOR ME / MY RULES FOR YOU

( ) MY RULES FOR ME / WHO CARES

( ) I DON'T KNOW / MY RULES FOR YOU

( ) MY RULES FOR ME / YOUR RULES FOR YOU

13) Action Level

When you come into a situation, do you usually act quickly after sizing it up, or do you do a de-

tailed study of all the consequences and then act?
( ) PROACTIVE
( ) REACTIVE
( ) INACTIVE

14) **Stress Response**
Tell me about a _____ situation that gave you trouble.

( ) THINKING
( ) FEELING
( ) CHOICE

15) **Attention Direction**
Do they react to others change in moods or do they ignore others changes around them.
( ) SELF
( ) OTHERS

16) **Time Orientation**
Recall a memory from your past. Pleas point to where this picture/thought cam from in space. (repeat question for a future event)

If you have an appointment with someone and they show up 15 minutes late, do you consider them to be late.

( ) THROUGH TIME – Left to right, On Time
( ) IN TIME – Front to back, Late

17) **Values**
In the context of Life, what's important to you? (List 9 or 10 things)
Rank them in order of importance.

18) IF you could fantasize aloud for a moment about the ideal _____ for you, what would it be?

19) Why did you leave your last _____?

20) If I were to call your former employer/partner and ask what they thought of you in your role as _____ what do you think they will tell us?

21) What are three things you like about yourself as it relates to _____?

22) What are three things you like least about yourself as it relates to _____?

23) What hobbies do you enjoy?

24) What do you look forward to in a _____?

Overview of Meta Program Survey -Things you should understand-

As you read through the comments about how the ideal recruit would respond to each questions keep in mind that these are generalizations and you will find exceptions.

Your job is to test it out for yourself and find **your** ideal recruit and house member.

1) *Criteria*
What do you want in a _____ *? List 3 to 6 things.*

All of the answers that you get like "fun", "security", "understanding" can act as personal anchors and trigger words that revivify the state that makes the context (in the blank line) important. You can use them with that individual later to demonstrate that you are fulfilling that need. When you have this information you can insert them in the **PMC** processes to make the process more personal.

2) **Direction**

What will having (their criteria) do for you?
( ) TOWARD – attain, achieve, goals, include, accomplish, solutions
( ) AWAY FROM   - avoid, get away from, evade, exclude

This determines if they are more motivated by moving **toward** something they like or by moving **away from** something they don't like. You will find exceptions to this but as a general rule your best recruits and initiates will have a strong **toward** meta program.

Additionally, to get compliance this information is useful because they are moving **toward** you let them know that they will get something when they follow along. If they are **away from,** you let them know that by following along they will avoid discomfort.

3) **Source**

How do you know that you have done a good job in _____? Do you know it inside, or does someone have to tell you?
( ) INTERNAL -Knows inside self
( ) MONSTLY INTERNAL, SOME EXTERNAL
( ) EXTERNAL – Told by Others
( ) MOSTLY EXTERNAL, SOME INTERNAL

For a recruit the more external the better. That will allow them to easily feel rewarded by your words and attention. As a house leader however you should respond with a high degree in internal.

4) **Reason**

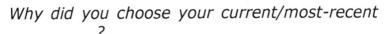

*Why did you choose your current/most-recent
_____?*
*( ) OPTIONS – Criteria, Look for other ways,
possibilities*
( ) MOSTLY OPTIONS, SOME PROCEEDURE
( ) PROCEEDURE – Necessities, Facts, The Way
( ) MOSTLY PROCEDURES, SOME OPTIONS

This one is fun. When you ask this question people will respond by either telling you a story of the process that lead them to the decision (PROCEDURE) or they will mention their criteria and talk about possibilities. Both are useful in how you present your information. All you need to do is to present your information to match their **Reason** meta-program.

For example, if the question is "How did you choose your current/most-recent job?"

A **procedures** response might sound something like "I went to a job fair with a friend and saw a booth that was about becoming a gourmet hot dog chef. I talked for a while and after thinking about it I thought that would be fun. I called the company up and got their information and went for a tour of the training facility and..."

A **reason** response might sound like "I wanted to find something to do that would involve cooking. I looked into everything from pastry cook to making fruit salad bowls. The gourmet hot dog company had the training and backing I wanted so I applied."

You'll notice that **procedures** is a story with a long narrative while **reasons** is filled with facts

5) **Relationship**

· What is the relationship between these three Boxes?

· What it the relationship between what you're doing this year and what you were doing last year?

· On average, how long have you stayed on a job/in a relationship?

( ) SAMENESS – Same thing, No Change, Similar

( ) SAMENESS /w EXCEPTION

( ) DIFFERENCE - Different, change, New, Unique

( ) DIFFERENCE /w EXCEPTION

Here you'll find out what method do they use to define relationships. Once you find that out, again you can tailor your presentation to fit their **Relationship** meta program by telling them "It's exactly like..." (SAMENESS) or "It different from ..." (DIFFERENCE).

When asking about this meta program it's important to **not** ask "What's the difference between these three squares?" or "How are these squares the same?" because you will suggest either difference or sameness. Keep the question about **relationship.**

6) **Convincer**

How do you know that a _____ is a good?

( ) SEE

( ) HEAR

( ) DO

( ) READ

Here you'll learn what your subject will need to see, hear, do or read in order to know if something, or someone is good. This is just the first step in know someone's "convincer strategy". The next step will follow.

7) *Convincer Demonstration*
How often do they have to demonstrate being good to you before you are convinced?
( ) _____ TIMES
( ) _____ LENGTH OF TIME
( ) AUTOMATIC
( ) CONSISTENT

When you know someone has to first see, hear, do or read something to be convinced that it's good, there is also a number of time it must happen to convince them **absolutely** that it's good. To get more details here is a full description of "the Convincer Strategy" that I found on the net:

The convincer Strategy quickly determines what a person requires in order to be convinced that something is good (or worth buying).

To elicit someone's convincer Strategy (this is so simple it will blow you away) you only have to ask two questions and follow some very simple rules.

Question #1 "How do you know _____ is good?"
After asking this question you will get one of four answers

1) "I have to *see it*."
2) "I have to *read about it*."

3) "I have to **hear about it**."
4) "I have to **do it/ feel it/work with it**."

None of these answers are wrong of course as each person has their own strategy for being convinced. When you hear their answer agree with it and remember what they said.

Once you have this response be prepared to deliver the information according to their answer.
If they must see it show it to them.
If they must read about it have written material for them read to read.
If they must hear about it be ready to introduce them to people who can give testimonials. If they must do or feel it have something ready for them with which they can interact.

Question #2 "How many times or for how long do you have to see it/read about it/hear about it/do it before you are convinced it's good?"

This is a vital part of the process. From this answer you will get four possible responses.

1) "I just have to see it/read about it/hear about it/do it **once** and I'm convinced."
2) "I have to see it/read about it/hear about it/do it **X number of times** and I'm convinced."
3) "I have to see it/read about it/hear about it/do it for **X length of time** and I'm convinced."
4) "I'm **never** convinced."

Regardless of which response you receive you have their personal process to be convinced and all that is needed is to fulfill their strategy. It's that simple.

Of course, there are numerous combinations so I'll give a few examples.

For Example, in and situation of a salesman selling widgets:

Salesman: How do you know a widget is good?

Prospect: I would have to read about it.

S: How much do you have to read to know a widget it good?

P: I'd have to see it's review in Widget Digest and do two or three internet searches on it.

S: Great, here is the Widget Digest that did our review and let me show you the search results here on my computer.

Salesman: How do you know a widget is good?

Prospect: I would have to try it for a while."

S: Great,. How long would it take you to try it? P: About a week.

S: Let me have you take this widget and you can have it for two weeks as part of our service package before you decide you want it."

Salesman: How do you know a widget is good?

Prospect: I would have to see it working.

S: How long would you have to see it working to know it's good?

P: I'm never convinced. I'd have to see it working EVERY TIME to be really convinced it's good.

What do you do now?

The answer, is future pace. It might go something like this.

Salesman: As you see it now do you notice it fulfills what you need right now, doesn't it?

Prospect: Yeah, Sure NOW it does.

S: Can you see it in your mind a week from now meeting the same needs and have that feelings?

P: Yeah, I suppose.

S: And you know where you'll be each time you see it can't you...have that feeling?

P: Okay yes I can.

The convincer Strategy is one way to really lock in a sale and it's also just ONE of the NLP meta program that you can use to powerfully influence people.

8) *Primary Sort*

Tell me about a vacation that you really enjoyed or what you think would be your ideal vacation. What did/would you like about it?

( ) PEOPLE
( ) PLACE
( ) THINGS
( ) ACTIVITY
( ) INFORMATION

How is this information useful? With it you can emphasize what they are most responsive to during your presentation.

Those prospects who tend to sort by people are likely to make very good recruits but the other responses are important too.

9) *Style*

Tell me about a _____ in which you were happiest (a one time event).

( ) INDEPENDENT – I, Sole responsibility, Myself, Alone

( ) PROXIMITY – With Others But In Control
( ) COOPERATIVE – All of Us, With Others, We,
Share Responsibility

This meta program will give you a way of predicting what situations they would best respond to by offering them the right range of autonomy or interdependence. For an ideal candidate for a house member they would likely mark COOPERATIVE.

10) *Chunk Size*
SPECIFIC: will talk with and about sequences.
Extra modifiers used. They use proper nouns.
GENERAL: Simple sentences, few modifiers. No
sequence, Steps let out. No proper nouns.

Some people need get many small details to feel as if they understand something, in which case they are *SPECIFC*. Others get a "big picture" view of something in order to understand it.

As a rule, when you are persuading you can present information to them to fit their chunk size. However when teaching it will increase their flexibility to encourage them to try to use the opposite of their chunk size.

Most people who are *SPECIFIC* set at the very front of the class room ready to soak up every bit if information. Those who are *GENERAL* tend be be at the very back of the room trying to get "the bigger picture".

11) *Modal Operators*
What do you say to yourself this morning
when you decided to get up?

(Circle one: Can, Have To, Must, Want, Gotta, etc.)

This is what they tell themselves to get motivates. Very Useful!

12) **Rule Structure**
What is a good way for you to increase your chances for success at a _____?
What is a good way for someone else to increase their chances?
Do you find it easy to tell them?
( ) MY RULES FOR ME / MY RULES FOR YOU
( ) MY RULES FOR ME / WHO CARES
( ) I DON'T KNOW / MY RULES FOR YOU
( ) MY FULES FOR ME / YOUR RULES FOR YOU

This will give you an idea of how well they will work with others. Expect some challenges with people who fall under the category of *I DON'T KNOW / MY RULES FOR YOU.*

13) **Action Level**
When you come into a situation, do you usually act quickly after sizing it up, or do you do a detailed study of all the consequences and then act?
( ) PROACTIVE
( ) REACTIVE
( ) INACTIVE

This will tell you how much responsibility people will willingly take on and how they react to stress caused by immediate change.

14) *Stress Response*
Tell me about a _____ situation that gave you trouble.

( ) THINKING
( ) FEELING
( ) CHOICE

This will let you know how they respond under stress and what their first reaction will most likely be. Thus you can give them assignments that emphasize this response by asking them to "Think it through." or "Give my your feelings on it." or "Describe the options that are available."

This question alone can be a very useful tool in a teaching situation to increase flexibility. To do this you create a hypothetical situation and ask each person to respond in a way that is NOT their standard mode of Stress Response.
Do this as an exercise on yourself to increase your flexibility.

15) *Attention Direction*
Do they react to others change in moods or do they ignore others changes around them.
( ) SELF
( ) OTHERS

You should ask this question but more importantly you should also observe the prospect as well. You can also ask them how do they respond when a close friend or partners mood changes.

For the purpose of "house" members it will benefit

to have people who are sensitive to others.

16) **Time Orientation**
Recall a memory from your past. Please point to where this picture/thought came from in space. (repeat question for a future event)

If you have an appointment with someone and they show up 15 minutes late, do you consider them to be late.

( ) THROUGH TIME – Left to right, On Time
( ) IN TIME – Front to back, Late

Those who are *THROUGH TIME* are good at focusing on how things are interconnected through time and are good at organizing past/present/future and make plans accordingly.

Those who are *IN TIME* are good quickly dealing with what needs to be done now.

17) **Values**
In the context of Life, what's important to you? (List 9 or 10 things)
Rank them in order of importance.

Very, VERY Important. These are their key values in life. They can be used very effectively to motivate and frame situation. There is a great deal of caution to be taken if you use this lightly because if you cannot fulfill those values to their satisfaction it is very likely they will feel cheated and betrayed and you will make an enemy for life.

18) If you could fantasize aloud for a moment

about the ideal _____ for you, what would it be?

Truly useful information. You will get their ideal fantasy of (context) . This does not mean that you have to fulfill it but the closer model you can create for them the stronger response you will get.

19) Why did you leave your last _____?

This will tell you what situations must occur or what rules must be broken to reach their threshold of acceptability.

20) If I were to call your former employer/partner and ask what they thought of you in your role as _____ what do you think they will tell us?

This will at least put them on guard. As an exercise it will demonstrate their degree of empathy. Note that if they respond with reflexive anger, defensiveness and avoid the question they are not very empathic – I would keep them at a distance.

21) What are three things you like about yourself as it relates to _____?

When ever you positively acknowledge these three things you reinforce good feelings.

These can be used as a carrot for motivation. You can also frame a task within the context as **"And you can (action/task) because you are (thing you like) and (thing you like) and (thing you like)."**

22) What are three things you like least about yourself as it relates to _____?

These can be used as a motivational "stick" to move away from a behavior. When a behavior/response occurs all that is needed is to frame the response in terms of any one of the things they like least about themselves. **"And you can (action/task) because you're NOT (thing you dislike) and (thing you dislike) and (thing you dislike)."**

23) What hobbies do you enjoy?

This gives you an idea of how they spend their idle time and thus where their mind naturally tends to lead them.

24) What do you look forward to in a _____?

Again, very useful. You are getting a motivational "carrot" with this information and you can use it to create a sense of anticipation.

Rapport vs. Compliance

There is a lot of talk in the persuasion and NLP community about rapport and how to gain it.

Yes, it is absolutely true what they say that "With rapport anything is possible and without it nothing is possible." Plenty of trainers have dedicated a LOT of seminar time to rapport building exercises like mirroring and matching.

That said, I want to go up a level and talk about what we are really wanting to achieve in persuasion and that is compliance.

Face it, if you are in a persuasion setting and have an outcome for someone, what you want them to be is COMPLIANT to your outcome. If you don't agree with that then LEAVE THIS PAGE NOW because it's a simple fact that a lot of "white lighters" would rather not face.

It is possible to have compliance without rapport and many have achieved that by threats, guilt, shame, guns to heads, and other less-than-positive behaviors but there are a more pleasant ways to gain compliance.

Ways to create compliance:

Assume authority

By presenting yourself as the authority in what you know and what you are doing people will tend to treat you accordingly.

* Ask for compliance

Bet you didn't think of that. Yes, you can do that by simply asking somehow. Example: *"I'd like to ask you to simply follow along here and give my your whole attention. No doubt a lot of people might have something else on their minds, so, for while I'm here would you be willing to put those things aside for the next 5 minutes?"*

* Build compliance

This is a old sales trick. The salesperson asks the prospect to sit in a different chair than the prospect is sitting in or use one pen instead of another. The salesperson then acknowledges the prospect each time he complies. One famous lecturer would frame success in his training as requiring a need for 'discipline' and, under that pretense, ask the audience to discipline themselves to stand up from their chair, turn around and sit down every time he snapped his fingers. After snapping he fingers every ten minutes during his 2 hour presentation he built a very compliant audience.

In the area of successful dating for men someone came up with the concept of the "mini-date" where the man would expose his date to several different environments in one date. This could include meeting at a coffee shop then going to a costume store to try on costumes and followed by a walk through an antique store or some unique part of town. All very cheap and creates an experience where the woman yields to the experience that the man creates, subtly creating compliance.

Perfected Mind Control – www.MindControl101.com

(I'd love to hear of any womans use of this technique.)

Now the same can also be applied in order to build rapport.

*Assume rapport
Present yourself as already being in rapport with your prospect.

*Ask for rapport
Not difficult. It could sound something like this *"Bob, I'm going to assume that I can feel comfortable talking with you today, like we're old friends talking business. For while we're here would you be willing to work from that same assumption?"*

*Build rapport
Learn rapport skills and USE THEM!

Now the difference between rapport and compliance is that, as a general rule, rapport is designed to effect the unconscious behaviors and compliance directs the conscious behaviors.

There have been some very effective persuaders and therapists who have relied solely on compliance, even to the point of breaking rapport, and still gotten good results. My advice USE EVERYTHING to get your outcome.

What internal quality does it take to build strong compliance? The best quality is a fearless belief that what you are doing. Or, as they explained in the movie "Glengarry Glen Ross", a set of brass balls.

The Wall, The Reed, The Water, The Wind. A
meditation in haiku form

The Wall

The   solid   wall   falls when struck by sufficient force. It's   strength holds weakness.

The Reed

The reed bends to wind
But will uproot to water.
Limiting it's give.

The Water

Rushing water flows
Mass Flooding Encompasses
The Valley contains it.

The Wind

The Wind surrounds all.
And yet it grasps at nothing.
Even lungs exhale.

These haikus are, of course metaphors, for our way of moving through the world. Many young and ambitious will work to build themselves strong and unyielding, The Wall.

Others will learn flexibility to one degree or another, The Reed, The Water.

Yet who can stop The Wind?

Some leaders rail at those who proclaim him as a cult of personality and like a samurai who slashes at the wind all one sees is the perspiration of his efforts.

Others step to the moral high ground to guard against evil NLP mind control yet people still want real power over others.

To change the world is futile. To be in it is everything.

Conclusion

Okay, there you have it.

My guess it that your response is one of shock, excitement, dismay and maybe even anger. If so, that's the purpose.

What you do with this information is now entirely up to you and I take no responsibility for the results you get. Don't be surprised when you get exactly what you want. Also, don't be surprised if what you thought you wanted wasn't quite what you expected.

My hope is that it's has given you a bigger picture of what is possible.

My only advice is to use the information for good constructive purposes and leave people feeling much better than you found them.

I wish you luck.

Sincerely,

Dantalion Jones

About the Author.

Because of the nature of his work Dantalion Jones seldom gives interviews. He has allowed himself to be interviewed once.

Here is a transcript of that inter- view.

The Editor

An Interview With Dantalion Jones

Dantalion Jones is the name of a self-proclaimed expert on Mind Control. His controversial blog http://Mindcontrol101.blogspot.com has created a small cult following among those who seek and fear the power of mind control.

This interview took place in February 2006.

William Mathis – Dantalion, you're a very difficult person to get in contact with.

Dantalion Jones - Yeah, I learned a long time ago that telling people that I teach mind control can be dangerous. As a result I decided that if I was going to be open about what I know I darn well have to cover my ass. You got lucky. I was in a good mood.

W M – I'd like to point out that to do this interview we had to agree not to discuss certain details about you.

Dantalion Jones – I appreciate that.

W M – What have been some of the consequences of you talking about mind control?

Dantalion Jones – On the good side, I've had the benefit of being approached by certain people who say they represent "government interests". That was interesting. So I got exposure to a few things most people suspected were true but could never confirm. On the down side, hate mail of course, and accusations that I've helped brainwash someones kid. But that's par for the course.

W M – When did your interest in mind control start?

Dantalion Jones – It started with books. There are plenty of them, some good, some crap. I've taken a lot of fluffy bunny hypnosis courses. When I heard about NLP a long time ago I started to take my suspicions seriously that people could be dramatically influenced through covert means.

W M – What did you do?

Dantalion Jones – I took a lot of the NLP trainings from some big names and I tested it out for myself. Made a huge number of mistakes and found out what works. I did hypnosis for a while. I'd also go out in social settings and see what I could get away with using conversational techniques. That taught me a lot.

W M – Who did you train under?

Dantalion Jones – I'd rather not say.

W M – What's your biggest discovery?

Dantalion Jones – That it's better to leave some people alone. Their too much bother.

W M – What do you mean?

Dantalion Jones – When I was testing out my theories I was pretty indiscriminate. I would try something with just about everyone I met. I'd get some sex crazed woman banging on my door at some god awful hour demanding my attentions and people calling me up thinking that if they take a bit of my time to hear my voice they'll feel better. Since then I've learned to qualify anyone I work with. I want to make sure they have some emotional stability and that all their ores are in the water. When I figured that out it saved me a lot of misery.

W M – How do you qualify them?

Dantalion Jones – I talk to them a while. There are a set of red flags that come up if they seem crazy. Things like abusive childhood, drug addiction. Let's see, if it's a married woman who wants to use me as an escape capsule from a bad marriage. Rigid thinkers. That's a few.

W M – Who does make a good prospect for you?

Dantalion Jones – If they are adventurous. A good sense of humor. Curious. I've found that if their fathers called them "princess". These tend to be good signs. But I take each person on a case by case basis.

W M – How do you think?

Dantalion Jones – (laugh) That's a good question. God, where do I start?

W M – Well, how do you deal with things when shit happens?

Dantalion Jones – I'm pretty jaded. I've managed to eliminate most surprises when people act out and stuff like that.

W M – How did you do that?

Dantalion Jones – It took a while. I've been through a lot of shit. Under the worst of stresses most people would either put up walls to protect themselves or curl up in a fetal position. I decided to apply what I knew about mind control on myself and become more flexible when BS happens.

W M – What does surprise you?

Dantalion Jones – The only thing that truly surprises me

is when someone is truly kind, genuine, giving and forgiving. I'm never ready for that.

W M – Do you have a lot sins to be forgiving?

Dantalion Jones – Don't we all? Some more than others?

W M – Have you met many people who surprise you like you describe?

Dantalion Jones– Not many. They are like a rare jewel in a coal mine.

W M – Dantalion, You write a lot about cults and especially how to form one. What's your person experience with cults?

Dantalion Jones – I've been through some of the personal growth seminars like Landmark Forum. That had some value to it. I lived in Europe for a while and sided up with a guy named Marco who had a house of about five to seven women. They would rotate in an out of his house sort of like a poorer version of Hugh Heffner. He boasted himself as a psychic but when he got drunk he would tell me some of his secrets. He used psychic reading and hypnosis to keep his house of women happy. I got interested in Scientology for a while because they talked about control- ling how you think but that quickly fell away when they began telling me how much it would cost to get
"clear". So I decided to see how far I could infiltrate the organization just using what I know.

W M – Did it cost you a lot of money?

Dantalion Jones – Less than I thought. I'd just move to a new city on the west coast and decided to walk in to one of their orgs as a trained auditor.

W M - What did you learn from your Scientology experience?

Dantalion Jones – It confirmed what I suspected. That most people are easier to control than they want to be- lieve. I did learn about their "training routines" first hand and saw how damned pliable people will be- come by going through "the gradient" of routines. It was something else. The whole Scientology idea of "getting clear" I realized was just a ploy to give peo- ple a problem they can focus on and their whole idea of ethics, they talk about that a lot, is a tool to pro- vide them with a sense of moral superiority. From a non-judgmental big picture point of view they've created self replicating meme that is quite impres- sive.

W M – How do you think the people close to you see you?

Dantalion Jones – Seriously, I'm a nice guy! I try to make sure that the people around me are as happy as pos- sible. Knowing what I do I can't be open about con- trolling peoples minds. So I would guess that some people think of me as a "man of mystery" and, I have to admit, that it's a façade that I've tried to cul- tivate.

W M – What's your biggest annoyance?

Dantalion Jones – I'd say it's peoples eagerness to blame and find excuses for their lives. I got a lot of that from the Landmark Forum type trainings but you don't need to shell out all that money to figure it out. Look, I'm the first to tell anyone that shit happens. There is a lot of things in life that are completely out of our control. There's nothing that we can do about it. But we do have one area where we can take con- trol and that is how we respond to the shit that hap- pens. I get a bit annoyed when I see people having some knee jerk emotional reaction over something that seems trivial. On the other hand, it's sort of amusing, like watching monkeys throw feces. They have no idea that they could choose a better re- sponse.

W M – What do you when they do that with you?

Dantalion Jones – I've got an air of smugness that I try to suppress. I stay calm, ask good questions and do my best to help them find a solution. I find a lot of peo- ple would much rather complain about the problem than work on a solution, so I let them vent. Monkeys throwing feces, remember?

WM – Are you saying you never get triggered or angry.

Dantalion Jones – I wish! That's another thing that surprises me, when I get caught up, angry. God knows, I haven't figured it all out. My life is a work in pro- gress. Maybe someday I'll get tired of this field of study and move on to gardening or making wicker baskets but till what I'm doing now amuses me.

W M – Any new mind control projects you're working on?

Dantalion Jones – I'm always working on something. Whether I make it available to the general public is another matter.

W M – Okay, well, what' the latest.

Dantalion Jones – I'm calling it "Perfected Mind Control" or **PMC** for short. I'm looking at the stuff that Robert J. Lifton wrote about in the 1960's on thought reform and old style brainwashing techniques that force people into compliance. I'm wanting to systematize a process I've developed that get the same results as traditional mind control but without any coercion or punishments. I want the people in the cult to be happy, healthy, and eager to please with no hint of intimidation or fear. It's a tall order.

W M – Have you tested it?

Dantalion Jones– Oh yeah! With some great results but I'm wondering if the world is ready for me to present it.

W M – How come? What's your main concern?

Dantalion Jones – Mostly that someone will not follow the instructions. My concern is that some hormone filled college student will think he's going to create his own harem using it and not correctly qualify the women he tries to recruit. It's a recipe for trouble. Another concern is that when people read it they begin to project all their own fears and issues about the abuse of power. I've shared it with a few people close to me and most of them get very very worried. I think they are seeing their own issues about how they might abuse power if they had it.

W M – So you say you've tested it. What did you learn?

Dantalion Jones – I learned a creative way to let people leave the cult that causes minimal discomfort. In fact they are not shunned and often take refuge from the world by returning for a while. So I think I've come across a nice way of doing what most people think of as mind control but without the so- called "bad" aspects.

WM – Any other projects?

Dantalion Jones -   There are few seeds of things that I've been thinking about but I'm not sure how they'll transpire. One is the idea that we're all trying to not be "thought criminals" as George Orwell put it and how to overcome societies long list of "shoulds" and live the life we want. It's thought provoking but I don't know how it will evolve, yet.

W M – What is your private life like.

Dantalion Jones – I'd rather not say.

Notes:

Perfected Mind Control – www.MindControl101.com

Made in the USA
Charleston, SC
19 March 2010